Life Purpose

Life Purpose

*In the right place,
At the right time,
With the right people.*

David Kalamen

Copyright ©2024 David Kalamen
ISBN 10: 1-988226-72-4
ISBN 13: 978-1-988226-72-9
All rights reserved.

Edited by Marion McKeown

Cover design by Nicole Wismann

Published by

First Page Publishing
Peachland, BC, Canada

Original paperback published by Twenty-Seven Soldiers Publishing Company, Kelowna, British Columbia, Canada in 2004 by David R. Kalamen with ISBN 0-9731826-0-1

Scripture quotations marked (AMP) are taken from the Amplified Bible, Copyright ©1954, 1958, 1962, 1964, 1965, 1987 by The Lockman Foundation. Used by permission.
Scripture quotations marked (NIV) are taken from the Holy Bible, New International Version® (NIV)®. Copyright ©1973, 1978, 1984 by International Bible Society. Used by permission of Zondervan.
All rights reserved.

The Message Translation by Eugene H. Peterson, Copyright ©1993, 1994, 1995, 1996, 2000. Used by permission of NavPress Publishing Group. All rights reserved.
Scripture quotations marked (KJV) are King James Version. Authorized King James Version.
Scripture quotations marked (NASB) are taken from the New American Standard Bible, Copyright ©1960, 1962, 1963, 1968, 1971, 1972, 1973, 1975, 1977 by the Lockman Foundation.
Used with permission.

Scripture quotations marked (NKJV) are taken from the New King James Version. Copyright ©1979, 1980, 1982, 1991 by Thomas Nelson, Inc. Used by permission. All Rights Reserved.
Limited use of any other scriptures are given credit accordingly.

My Testimony

It was the fall of 1971. I was a healthy nineteen-year old in my second year of Bible College training and about to ask a very special lady if she would be my bride. I had just come home from playing ball hockey when my life was knocked for a loop. Within twenty-four hours I was lying in a hospital bed in North Vancouver's Lions Gate hospital with extensive internal bleeding.

Without delay the doctors had X-rays in their hands and were pointing to a tumor attached to my right kidney. My surgeon's evaluation was that the tumor was a very active, cancerous growth. This meant an operation was necessary immediately, with the possibility of removing the kidney. My parents were contacted and they arrived in Vancouver greatly concerned about my welfare.

I can still remember lying awake that night. As my thoughts raced back and forth, I recalled the night that I had responded to an altar call at a youth convention two years previously. I had gone to the front to have it out with God. My heart had been filled with confusion and frustration over His silence regarding my life.

God was merciful. In a moment of time the hardness of my heart was softened and the confusion was removed. He spoke to me in an audible voice and said, "David, I am calling you into the ministry as a teacher: go to Bible school." It was such a clear directive and so quickly confirmed with a word of knowledge by a visiting guest speaker that I immediately obeyed and pursued the training I needed to prepare for the ministry. God came through!

Now, here I was, just two years into a three-year Bible program, lying on a hospital bed and facing what would become one of my greatest tests. I was a young man. I didn't want to die. I wanted to marry and have children. I wanted to live a full life. A life that had been filled with such incredible possibilities the day before, now felt so defrauded by this new reality. What was going to happen to me?

I had experienced a rich Christian heritage. I had seen God work in supernatural power. I had known His merciful dealings in my life, but that was then and this was now! I felt a sense of desperation. The rush surgery was scheduled for the following morning. I needed a Word from the Lord to enter into my troubled heart and mind.

I opened my Bible to 1 Samuel and began to read about the life of a young man called David. I had heard this story many times, but that night the Holy Spirit began to open my spirit to a revelation and insight of scripture that was new and fresh. A rhema word was deposited into my heart and spirit concerning His purpose for my life.

I read about Samuel, the prophet, calling and anointing David to be the king who would replace

Saul's rule over Israel (1Sa 16). I had been called and anointed to teach the gospel. I could relate to this divine commissioning.

Then I read about David's journey to see his brothers at the battlefront. He saw great fear as not one of Israel's men would respond to the challenge to fight Philistia's champion, Goliath. Well, I was also facing my own giant and it was producing within me the kind of anxiety that must have been brewing within David's brothers.

As I continued reading about David defeating Goliath on the battlefield, I was awe-struck with a question that opened up my heart to God: "What made David, a young man, a shepherd, so courageous and so confident of victory in warfare?" His actions almost appeared presumptuous and foolhardy. After all, he was facing a seasoned, well-trained warrior.

But David had a history and the weapon of a testimony. He had experienced divine protection and deliverance when he faced the jaw of a lion and the paw of a bear (1Sa 17). I could identify with David. I was a hunter and enjoyed the wilderness, but I wouldn't want to face a panther or grizzly bear without the aid of a high-powered rifle. How could he have faced these animals with a sling and a staff? But he did, and won. "What made him so courageous and so confident of victory?" I needed to know.

David's motivations appear carnal at best: "What shall be done for the man who kills this Philistine and takes away the reproach of Israel?" (1Sa 17). However, after Samuel anointed him, the "Spirit of the Lord came mightily upon him from that day forward" (1Sa 16.13). Nowhere does it point to him being changed into another man as Saul had been (1Sa 10.6). What was his secret?

That night God revealed to me a life-giving principle. The secret lay in David's covenantal perspective of God. He had a covenant with God. It was not a general covenant lodged in the rite of circumcision alone but a specific covenant lodged in Samuel's prophetic Word, to David, that he was to be Israel's next king.

David's courage and confidence rested in his personal awareness and knowledge of his life purpose and destiny in God. That had to be it!

I believe that David felt secure that he could not die until God's purpose for his life was fulfilled. He was not king yet and the Word of the Lord had not yet come to pass; so, he could not die. Even though Goliath was a threat to the nation of Israel (1Sa 17), David was going to be their next king. Goliath would have to be removed for God's purpose to be fulfilled. So David ventured out to confront the giant, Goliath, in the confidence of his calling, anointing, and divine commissioning. He believed the prophet and so he prospered (11Ch 20.20).

That night this truth entered into my heart and set me free. I, too, could face my Goliath of cancer because God had called me to teach and I had not yet fulfilled my purpose. I was in training for the ministry, just like David was being trained for kingship. I could face my giant with courage and confidence, knowing that I was not going to die until the purpose He had revealed for my life was completed.

I cannot communicate the joy and faith that emerged from the depth of my spirit. The Word of the Lord quickened me and brought me life. I pulled the curtains around my bed and worshiped. During the next morning's surgery, the medical team searched for more than two hours for a tumor that had somehow vanished. The sword of the Spirit, the Word of God, had defeated my giant!

A life message emerged out of those days which I call life purpose. It is rooted into a life verse: "And we know that in all things God works for the good of those who love Him, who have been called according to His purpose" (Ro 8.28, NIV).

I'm Forever Grateful

To my Heavenly Father, to my elder brother Jesus, and to my helper, Holy Spirit, for making my life significant and for giving me the privilege and joy of portraying the Father's Heart for this generation, thank you.

To my parents, Arnold and Audrey Kalamen, who gave me life, introduced me to the One who has become my Life, and who have continually upheld this work in intercession, thank you.

To my precious wife, Carleen, who has experienced with me the fire and the flood in my journey to know God and to make Him known, and who has been my greatest friend and encouragement for 31 years, thank you.

To my children, Brodie, Ryan and Kerri, who have always challenged me to search myself and my understanding of God so that my faith could be relevant to the children of generations, and who have themselves integrated these same principles into their lives, thank you.

To my pastoral and leadership teams, office staff, and congregation of Kelowna Christian Center, who have stayed faithful to the upward call and have been willing to risk misunderstanding so that the greater purposes of God could be established in them, thank you.

To Marion McKeown (Mimi McQ), for her own example of a passionate pursuit of purpose through very difficult times, for her writing and resource skills, for her heart to sacrificially undertake and guide this project to completion, and for her friendship and perseverance in assisting me to place this life message in written script, thank you.

To you, the reader, friends I have not yet met, who have just opened this book and are willing to open your hearts to a revelation of His purposes and are willing to pay the price of knowing and doing His will, thank you.

CONTENTS

Chapter One: A Call to This Generation............ 1
Chapter Two: The Era of Post-Modernity.......... 7
Chapter Three: How Did We Get Here?............ 17
Chapter Four: Solomon: A Post-Modern Man?. 31
Chapter Five: An Identity Crisis........................ 39
Chapter Six: A Father's Heart............................ 57
Chapter Seven: You've Been On My Mind.......... 66
Chapter Eight: Getting to Know You................. 72
Chapter Nine: What Are You Doing, Lord?........ 92
Part Ten: You Called, God?............................... 114
Chapter Eleven: Where Did You Say We're Going?.. 125
Chapter Twelve: Knowledge of Divine Intention 138
Chapter Thirteen: I Did It On Purpose.............. 160
Chapter Fourteen: Marching Orders................. 165
Chapter Fifteen: A Word For All Seasons.......... 187
Chapter Sixteen: Understanding the Mysteries of Life Through the Eye of Purpose.................... 205
Chapter Seventeen: Principles of Purpose......... 213
Chapter Eighteen: Delightful Daily Disciplines. 236
Chapter Nineteen: Master Keys........................ 279
Chapter Twenty: Cheering On The Church!...... 294
About The Author.. 301

XIII

David Kalamen

Chapter 1

A Call to This Generation

Wake up, sleepy head!"

"How many times can a man hear a wake-up call without waking up?"

Stu Weber

"Answering the call of your Creator is the ultimate why for living."

Os Guiness

"Hosea put it well: "I'll call nobodiesand make them somebodies; I'll call the unloved and make them beloved. In the place where they yelled out, 'You'renobody!' they're calling you 'God's living children.'" Isaiah maintained this same emphasis: "If each grain of sand on the seashore were numbered and the sum labeled 'chosen of God,' they'd be numbers still, not names; salvation comes by personal selection."
Romans 9.25-27, *The Message Translation*

Faith Popcorn makes this wonderful statement in

her book called *The Popcorn Report:* "Once in a great while, events or innovations electrify the world in a way that permeates and transforms everyday life. The Industrial Revolution. [The Kennedy assassination]. Wars [Desert Storm 2], plagues [AIDS]. The invention of the car. Television. The micro-chip. [The cell]" (page 3, brackets mine).

And the list doesn't stop there. Anyone watching events unfold in the early 21st century would surely have to admit that things are never going to be as they once were. It was now an end to the age of innocence and the beginning of a century of fear and suspicion. As Casey Stengel put it: *"The future ain't what it used to be."*

> **"The future ain't what it used to be."**
> Casey Stengel

Sociologists have defined that what we are experiencing is a socioquake because of the sudden impact and the broad ripple effect that these changes are having on our society, our daily routine, and to our basic philosophy of life. We can feel these quake shifts taking place in every corner of the globe.

Even the Church is feeling the shaking. C. Peter Wagner, one of the most widely recognized authorities in the field of church growth, resonates with this thinking. He wrote a book entitled Churchquake! stating, *"The greatest change in the Church since the Protestant Reformation is taking place before our eyes"* (back cover).

New frontiers of the spirit are opening up every day. There are major denominational realignments happening almost everywhere. New networks are occurring on every level: we even see it in the emergence of new company and business partnerships. Yes, the face of Christianity is changing, but it seems the entire world is experiencing a prophetic shift.

We are experiencing the death throes of a dying century. We are praying that there is life after death. People are looking for that tangible something that used to anchor generations gone by. This is a mainstream and not a fringe movement.

Even Faith Popcorn has understood this social swing. She states in her book *Clicking*: "The bad news: our society is adrift. The good news: it's still afloat! Even though we have been tossed about on the sea of life—our values, morals and ideals battered and bashed—we're renewing our spirits by grabbing on to a hope-line, a connection that anchors our spiritual core. After several decades of materialism and meanness, we are looking for simple answers once again: 'Yes,' we're saying, 'You can take away outer layers—my job, my wallet, my car—but you can't squash my inner spirit'" (page 105).

All across the spectrum we are observing a generation that is honestly searching for meaning that transcends the material, the corporeal, and the temporary. People are actively looking for new solutions to old questions and the very act of looking is an encouraging sign of spiritual hunger.

Life Purpose

People are presently returning to religion en masse, but are not necessarily embracing established religion: to many of them, the established religious culture is a part of the problem. Therefore, they have rejected any previous spiritual landmarks and are now looking elsewhere for guidance and direction.

They are currently entering into an age of mysticism. There is a very strong belief in a higher power (84%), in miracles (76%), in life after death (63%), in Satan (51%), or out-of-body experiences (46%).

We are most definitely living in a transitional generation between what was and what will be, because it appears that a millennial generation—purposeless and passionless—has emerged without any meaningful answers to the most critical questions of life:

- Who am I?
- Why am I here?
- What am I supposed to do?
- Where am I going?

Some generational specialists have called this generation, *Generation X*. The youth appear to have lost their way and are wandering in terms of purpose. They are displaying the fruit of a disease that is already in the root system of a society.

> *"The bad news: our society is adrift. The good news: it's still afloat!"*
> Faith Popcorn

Our young people are suffering from the broken promises and fading dreams of the preceding generations; institutional religion; divorce; violence; suicide; drugs; isolation and loneliness; violent forms of sexuality. Some people have more recently referred to these youths as *"echo boomers."*

Not that long ago a guest on the Dave Rutherford radio talk show in Canada summed up echo boomers this way: *"Our uniqueness starts with the fact that we have no uniqueness. We are whiners with little cause. We are lost, lazy, and clueless. We are spoiled and apathetic."*

After reading all this, it is not surprising Faith Popcorn said that we have become *"a nation looking to regain its lost soul"* (*Clicking,* page 112).

There is no doubt about it. The Church is facing an immense challenge. There is great disagreement about whom or what God is, what actually constitutes worship, and what the true values of life really are.

This is why God has appointed the Church to be an Issachar company of people who are able to *"understand the times"* (1Ch 12.32) we are in and know what we should be doing. We are being forced into brailling the culture and then feeling our way through the complexity of changes and the effect they are having on our culture, relying upon the Holy Spirit to help us to read the culture and awaken the soul of a sleeping generation to Him.

God desires that each one of us seek Him for the keys that will unlock the hearts of our peers, helping them to locate their life purpose and destiny. If God's

Life Purpose

people do not take this divine calling seriously, a generation could be lost.

Whatever trail humanity follows, we are experiencing a trend that the Church, its leaders, and ministries simply cannot ignore. There is a new breed of people coming forth, a *"chosen generation"* who know Christ and are not afraid of the cause or the cost of the cross (1Pe 2.9).

To quote Faith Popcorn once again, *"We are all at the start of a great awakening, a time of spiritual and religious revival"* (*Clicking*, page 112).

> **"I will go anywhere, provided it be forward."**
> Os Guiness

David Kalamen

Chapter 2
The Era Of Post-Modernity
"The Power of Choice"

A certain professor on entering his classroom always bowed deeply to his scholars. One day a friend of the professor accompanied him to his class, and after seeing him bow to the scholars, asked him, "Why do you do that?" The professor replied: "It is not just those boys I bow to, but to the men of the future that they will become."

Francis Gay, *The Friendship Book (1978)*

"I am who God says I am;
I can have what God says I can have;
I can do what God says I can do;
I can go where God says I can go;
I am and I can because HE IS!"

Personal identity comes through a capacity to extend backwards and forwards in time, and all at the same time. I can remember the past and make plans for the future. I have a place in history within the larger context of my personal relationships: to God; to my family; to people within my community; and to other people in my world.

Life Purpose

Imagine a generation where all of these roots have been severed, a generation where looking back makes them angry and looking ahead makes them reach the depth of despair. Also imagine, for a moment, a generation that does not have a meta-narrative, living life as a play without a central plot, both individually and corporately. Now imagine a generation without an ability to form authentic relationships, a generation that has lost absolutely any meaningful concept of a personal God, spirituality, or morality.

> **People are craving roots.**

That is an extremely accurate picture of our modern society. People are craving roots, purpose, intimate relationships, true spirituality, and ecological stability. Instead, they have been grazing in the field of evolution, family dysfunction, relational upheaval, spiritual confusion, and moral relativism. Our society, as a whole, has been obsessed with the spirit of what is being called *"post-modernity."* Let me clarify what this means.

The Pre-Modern era (up to the 18th Century) was mainly dominated by a *single religion, Christianity.* It was assumed that God existed and He could be known through the Church. The major belief system of this era? *"There is a God; therefore, I am."* The creature (man) was an extension of the Creator (God). A man's identity, purpose, and destiny derived from a personal knowledge of one person: God.

The Modern Era (18th Century to the 1970s) was mainly dominated by Enlightenment thinking which was built upon the idea that a universal set of truths could be uncovered by human reasoning, thought, and pursuit. This particular era believed in the continual ascent of man (fueled by Darwinian and Freudian thinking) and was greatly influenced by a *single dogma, secular progress*—"God doesn't exist because we have no scientific proof that He does." The central belief system? *"I think; therefore, I am."* The creature was independent of any Creator and had to decide his own identity, choose his own purpose, and trust in making his own destiny. Man determines his own existence and the meaning of life.

The Post-Modern Era (1970s on) has these characteristics:

No meta-narrative—all of the big ideas, faiths, ideologies, philosophies, technologies, and '-isms' have collapsed. They are no longer to be followed or adhered to without question, nor do they constitute the primary answer to the questions that surround the mystery of life. No single plot line of history is the true one. As a result of this shift, we are beginning to see some massive inter-faith conversions—for example, defections from the Hindu faith to Buddhism, and so on.

No objective morality—every view on life is relative and there is no such thing as absolute truth: all truth is viewed as being personal and independently held as opinion, as something that may be true for one but not true for the other; all truth is an idea, where, like in the movies, fiction and non-fiction blur.

Life Purpose

No meaningful long-lasting relationships—William Mahedy says in his book A Generation Alone that people have reached an emotional critical mass through relational trauma. Abortion, divorce, and also a transient family system have all contributed to a sense of disconnection and to a belief that no permanent relationship is possible. Too many of the relational foundations of society have collapsed and this has brought a generation into ruin.

No community identity—city dwellers have lost the stories that made the community. There has been a loss of continuity and identity in employment which has led to this generation's expectation of a series of varied, short-term posts and also an acceptance of a lower standard of living versus a career. It is sad that this generation *"cannot see themselves ever owning a nice home."*

No dream—very unlike *"The American Dream,"* it appears the post-modernists have little value of history (they can be ashamed and angered by it) and very few have a dream to dream. The memorable "I have a dream" messages of the Martin Luther King's belong to the past. It is not "what will I be when I grow older?" but *"if I grow older."*

> **It is not "what will I be when I grow older?" but "if I grow older."**

No confidence in the present social and moral code—they have seen religious leaders fail and fall. And they have also seen institutions fill with scandal and lose their credibility (for instance, Enron; the Lewinsky affair; Whitewater; the Los Angeles Police battering; racism). Few believe the codes really work and actually prefer not to seek new codes.

No time for the future—they are caught up with activities that celebrate immediacy ("Now!"). They are fascinated with the body: how it looks (fashion), how it feels (experiential), and the appetites of the present. Thoughts of the future are replaced with a preoccupation with fantasy. Hollywood has read the culture very well and is financing the emergence of a new fantasy culture.

This post-modern era is dominated by a single impulse, personal choice. Opinions have become the hallmark of a new culture and they are having the desired affect: truth has been repackaged for sale to a new generation. The prevailing belief system? *"I choose; therefore, I am."* This philosophy says, *"God may exist and it is up to everyone to find God as they believe Him to be."* There really is the advent of a new breed of agnostic and also the emergence of a society based upon personal opinion and choice.

Time Magazine has described this post-modern people as *Generation X*. The widely-read weekly magazine offered the following analysis about them:

> "They have trouble making decisions. They would rather hike the Himalayas than climb the corporate ladder. They have few heroes, no anthems, and no style to call their own. They crave entertainment, but their attention

Life Purpose

span is as short as the zap of a TV dial. They hate Yuppies, hippies, and druggies. They postpone getting married because they dread divorce. They possess only a hazy sense of their own identity, but also a monumental preoccupation with all the problems the preceding generation will leave them to fix" [for example, national indebtedness, the environmental problems, and high unemployment]."

As Ron Luce so aptly states in his book *Inspire the Fire: "This is a generation that lacks the zest to pour their lives into anything . . . there seems to be no battle cry."*
Many young people believe they will have a harder time accomplishing their parents' standard of living (so are staying home longer: for example, average 23-25 years of age). The music of the day is a remake of tunes from previous decades or the grunge rock which sounds like a lot of noise, buzz, and angry lyrics (the lyrics reflect hopelessness, death, suicide, anger, and apathy). They have not found a cause worth living, or dying for.
Don't despair! No matter how hopeless this sounds in the natural and no matter how disillusioned this generation may be, God has a plan and purpose for them that will affect history. He will not divorce Himself from their plight. He is prepared to touch the heart of this generation and give it a soul. He is ready

to pour out His Spirit and give them a *now* experience of His grace, power, and direction.

Like *Esther,* young women can grow up knowing they have "come to the kingdom for such an occasion as this" (Est 4.14).

> **"This is a generation that lacks the zest to pour their lives into anything."**
> Ron Luce

Like *Daniel,* young men can "know their God, be strong (*in their character*), and do exploits" for Him (Da 11.32, italics mine, KJV).

Like *King David,* we can eagerly look forward to seeing a generation leave this legacy: "after he had served God's will and purpose and counsel in his own generation, fell asleep [in death]" (Ac 13.36).

What God told Jeremiah's generation, he also says to this generation: "For I know the thoughts and plans that I have for you . . . thoughts and plans for welfare and peace, and not for evil, to give you hope in your final outcome" (Jer 29.11, AMP).

It is in knowing His plans and purposes that confidence for life and good emerge. Without Him, humanity is demeaned, life is devalued, and *Gen-Xers* emerge without their own identity, purpose, or destiny. With Him, a generation of the cross emerges with God-esteem, clarity of direction, and vision. It really doesn't take much for this generation to move from an *X* to a cross.

Thankfully, the search for wonder is back. *Gen-Xers* are looking for a sign they can follow, and I am convinced that whoever gives them hope and a future will ultimately affect their destiny. The Church of today cannot stand by, apathetic and uninvolved, when Jesus Christ is the solution and we have the answers. As Ron Luce says, *"Let's transform Generation X into a generation that stands for the cross."*

Comment: In my opinion *Generation X* is representative of an assembling of all generations into one.

The Spirit of Post-Modernity

The Bible states that the material, outer, temporal world is but a reflection of the supernatural and eternal world (Heb 11.3). What happens in the inner world of the spirit and character is then revealed in the outer world of the flesh and personality. So it is with society as a whole. Sin in society is a symptom of sin in the individual.

Properly discerning the spirit behind a generation is the Christian's business through the *"gift of discernment of spirits"* (1Co 12.10). Daniel 2.21 says, "He changes times and seasons; He sets up kings and deposes them. He gives wisdom to the wise and knowledge to the discerning" (NIV). This world has a god (2Co 4.4) and demonic spirits influence the lives of people in it (Eph 2.2-3). These spirits desperately want to impact every born-again Christian (1Jn 2.15-17) and infiltrate the Church of Jesus Christ, making it ineffective.

God points out that we are "not ignorant of the strategies of the devil" (2Co 2.11). The discerning Christian can stay fully alert to any deceptive spirit by staying separate from polluting influences and seductive doctrines, and yet, create a message that touches the heart of a generation and turns them to God. He or she can respond confidently to this divine shift taking place today and not drift.

In order for the Church of Jesus Christ to be healthy, there are spiritual trends and influences that it will have to address. I have recognized *three* major ones.

The first force is a *spirit of escapism*. The *drive to escape* is rooted in a lack of direction and purpose—we serve a God of purpose who has created us on purpose, for purpose.

> **Jesus Christ is the solution: His Church has the answers**

The second force is a *spirit of selfishness*. The ever on-going *drive to pamper self* is rooted in a loss of personal identity—the great I AM can tell us who we are and what we can be.

The second force is a *spirit of selfishness*. The ever on-going *drive to pamper self* is rooted in a loss of personal identity—the great I AM can tell us who we are and what we can be. The third major force is a *spirit of confusion*. The *drive to understand truth* is deeply rooted in a core absence of spiritual values—the Spirit of Truth can teach us truth and establish

Life Purpose

life values, dealing with a spirit of confusion. We need to fight spirit with Spirit and also with spiritual weapons (2Co 10.3-5). We are not dealing with individuals, age groups, music idols, or media personalities: we are dealing with a spirit that is focused on the destruction of a generation (Jn 10.10). Through the anointing of the Holy Spirit, God will impart His discernment, understanding, and authority that will enable us to start rebuilding and restoring the "devastation of generations" (Isa 61.4). We must activate the weapons that we have been given in order to counteract these strategies of the enemy to break and destroy the spirit of this present generation.

> *"Don't part company with your future. It is an anchor in the storm. A purposeless life is an early death. What you believe about your mission in life is the force that determines what you will accomplish or fail to accomplish in life."*
> John Mason

Chapter 3
How Did We Get Here?

God said, "Let us make man in our image."
Man said, "Let us make God in our image."

Douglas Jerrold

"A Rabbi and a soap maker went for a walk together. The soap maker said, "What good is religion? Look at the trouble and misery in the world after thousands of years of religion. If religion is true, why should this be?" The Rabbi said nothing. They continued walking until he noticed a child, filthy with mud and grime, playing in the gutter. The Rabbi said, "Look at the child. You say that soap makes people clean. We have had soap for generations. Yet look how dirty that child is. Of what value is soap?" The soap maker protested. "But, Rabbi, soap can't do any good unless it is used." "Exactly," replied the Rabbi.

Anonymous

The Apostle Paul makes it clear in Romans 1.18-32 that Christians must never neglect their relationship

Life Purpose

to the Creator, or forget that we are his handiwork. To do so opens the door to a downward moral spiral into depravity and vanity of life. This is the first generation that has been raised almost exclusively on an evolutionary concept of life. Is it any wonder that sociologists are talking about an emerging generation that is totally devoid of an identity and purpose?

The Message Translation adds weight to this scripture:

> "But God's angry displeasure erupts as acts of mistrust and wrong doing and lying accumulate, as people try to put a shroud over truth. But the basic reality of God is plain enough. Open your eyes and there it is! By taking a long and thoughtful look at what God has created, people have always been able to see what their eyes as such can't see: eternal power, for instance, and the mystery of His divine being. So nobody has a good excuse.
> What happened was this: People knew God perfectly well, but when they didn't treat him like God, refusing to worship Him, they trivialized themselves into silliness and confusion so that there was neither sense nor direction left in their lives. They pretended to know it all, but were illiterate regarding life. They traded the glory of God who holds the whole world in his hands for cheap figurines you can buy at any roadside stand.
> So God said, in effect, "If that's what you want, that's what you get." It wasn't long before they

were living in a pigpen, smeared with filth, filthy inside and out. And all this because they traded the true God for a fake god, and worshiped the god they made instead of the God who made them—the God we bless, the God who blesses us. Oh, yes!

Worse followed. Refusing to know God, they soon didn't know how to be human either—women didn't know how to be women, men didn't know how to be men. Sexually confused, they abused and defiled one another, women with women, men with men—all lust, no love. And then they paid for it, oh, how they paid for it—emptied of God and love, godless and loveless wretches.

Since they didn't bother to acknowledge God, God just quit bothering them and let them run loose. And then all hell broke loose: rampant evil, grabbing and grasping, vicious backstabbing. They made life hell on earth with their envy, wanton killing, bickering and cheating.

Look at them: they're mean-spirited, venomous, fork-tongued God-bashers. Bullies, swaggerers, insufferable wind bags! They keep inventing new ways of wrecking lives. They ditch their parents when they get in the way. Stupid, slimy, cruel, cold-blooded. And it's not as if they don't know better. They know perfectly well they're spitting in God's face. And they don't care—worse, they hand out prizes to those who do the worst things best!"

Life Purpose

Devolution, Not Evolution

Outside of acknowledging the Creator God, human life becomes void of purpose. To the secularist, the humanist and the evolutionist, life is the result of fate, circumstances, or what has become known as the *evolution of the species* (Darwin). Isn't it interesting that this present generation sees themselves as *survivors,* to highlight a popular millennial television show?

Evolution has been taught universally as a science in many educational circles. Evolution is not a fact; it is a theory. It is an intricate assimilation of such a vast number of theories that when people ask if I believe in the theory of evolution, I have responded by asking, *"Which theory?"*

These theories have been adopted as a fundamental belief system by our society, and their acceptance has created quite an epidemic of purposeless and passionless people of all ages.

I personally believe that the theory of evolution has *three* major problems.

> **Man has rejected the concept of a living Creator for moral, not scientific reasons.**

Firstly, it flies in the face of the *law of entropy* (the second law of thermodynamics) that specifies all order is deteriorating to disorder, chaos, and randomness.

20

Secondly, it flies in the face of *fossil records* that do not demonstrate any transitional forms (after 135 years of very intense research).

Thirdly, it flies in the face of *statistical probability*—there is no way that life could have developed from random chance (10 to the 262 just to form a single cell or a protein molecule).

D.J. Futuyma adds further fuel to this debate by offering this analysis:

> "Creation or evolution, between them, exhaust the possible explanation for the origin of life. Organisms appeared fully formed or they did not. If they did not, they developed. If they did, they must have been created by some Omnipotent intelligence" (*Science on Trial*, 1983, page 197).

How about those of us in North America? Have we removed God from our thinking? Has our natural thinking become godless, darkened by unbelief and agnosticism? I believe that it has, and one of the most powerful forces behind this godlessness [and consequently the search for significance] in our society is the evolution of *evolutionary thinking!*

What began with men like Erasmus, Darwin, and the Lunar Society as a theory concerning man's origin was then translated into the following streams of thought:

Life Purpose

A political ideology (includes Karl Marx, Atheistic and Dialectic Communism);

An educational philosophy (Alexander Dewie and the Humanist Manifesto—encourages the quest for the good life, believes man's primary responsibility and accountability is to himself, and that he has no need of a Saviour);

A new morality called moral relativity (Joseph Fletcher and Situational Ethics). Society has separated itself from the plumbline that measures every aspect of its authority. It has departed from its moral moorings and is dangerously afloat and adrift. Its morality has been left to the polling whims and moral fluctuations of each generation as they try to determine truth and value.

What is acceptable to the majority now becomes 'normality.' Normality is later viewed and skewed as 'moral!' What is seen as moral, by most, usually winds up being declared legal.

To oppose such a system requires a devout and very radical commitment by individuals or groups such as the Church. Protestantism definitely needs to re-emerge. Why? Because within time, resistance to the status quo will be considered anti-social, an abnormal belief system and behaviour, immoral, and in the long term very illegal;

Another stream of thought is expressed through *a new world religion called New Age* where men think they can become all the god that they need, the end product of a new genetic pool that is riding the crest of the last evolutionary stage on the verge of creating a super species, where the evolution of the mind has displaced the evolution of the body.

> **"Life must go on—I forget why."**
> Edna St. Vincent

Listen to some of the philosophical thinking that has emerged from an evolutionary base:

Edna St. Vincent—"Life must go on—I forget why."

Jean-Paul Sartre—"Every existence is born without reason, prolongs itself out of weakness, and then dies by chance!"

Voltaire—"You must go on living solely to enrage those who are paying your annuities. It is the only pleasure I have left!"

Count Leo Tolstoy—"The meaningless absurdity of life is the only incontestable knowledge accessible to man!"

Albert Camus—"It is clear that life will be lived all the better if it has no meaning."

Sigmund Freud—"The goal of all life is death."

Speak those life-producing statements to yourself on a daily basis and you will soon agree with Henry David Thoreau that *"most men lead lives of quiet desperation."*

Life Purpose

The Message Translation's introductory to the Book of Ecclesiastes adds more weight to these very depressing quotes. The *Quester* says:

> "Unlike the animals, who seem quite content to simply be themselves, we humans are always looking for ways to be more than or other than what we find ourselves to be. We explore the countryside for excitement, search our souls for meaning, shop the world for pleasure. We try this. Then we try that. The usual fields of endeavour are money, knowledge, power, adventure, and sex. Everything we try is so promising at first! But nothing ever seems to amount to very much. We intensify our efforts but the harder we work at it, the less we get out of it. Some people give up early and settle for a humdrum life. Others never seem to learn, and so they flail away through a lifetime, becoming less and less human by the year, until by the time they die there is hardly enough humanity left to compose a corpse."

People live that kind of life because they refuse to acknowledge God, His existence, His personhood, and also His personality. Life devolves into a pit of despair with that kind of thinking: it truly evolves when God is known and honoured for who He is.

Honouring God Leads to an Upward Call

I am very aware that people never change their belief system until their belief system fails to produce the desired effect. I believe that this generation is ready for a new belief system; one that affirms they were not born by accident, but on divine purpose. They were not born by chance, but by His choice. A belief that God has a special place in His heart for each of them, now and forever more.

It is very interesting to note here that despite the many inroads of evolutionary thinking, all of humanity innately acts as if they have supreme value. This is because the theories of evolution are countered by a belief that God exists and He is a rewarder of any of those who will earnestly and diligently seek Him [out].

> ***This generation is ready for a new belief system.***

Scripture gives us three realities as a counter to the theories of evolution. When we diligently seek Him, He reveals Himself through the act of creation (Ro 1); the fact of conscience (Ro 2); and the face of Christ (Ro 3).

Life Purpose

The Act of Creation

There is a divine design to the world. As a matter of fact, many present-day scientists are asking this probing question: *"Is mankind a central product of the universe? Or merely an accident to survive?"* (*Nature's Destiny* by Michael J. Denton, inside cover). Denton answers a resounding *"Yes!"* By the way, this is Michael's second book following his previous work *Evolution: A Theory in Crisis* (1984).

Paul Davies, another well-respected scientist and writer, pointed out in his book Accidental Universe (1982) that *"the impression of design is overwhelming"* (see Preface). It has become clearer to scientists that the older teleological religious concept of the cosmos as a specifically designed whole with life and mankind as its primary goal and purpose is consistent with our modern day research.

Listen to what King David so eloquently expressed in Psalm 19 (TMT):

> "God's glory is on tour in the skies, God-craft on exhibit across the horizon. Madame Day holds classes every morning. Professor Night lectures each evening. Their words aren't heard, their voices aren't recorded, but their silence fills the earth: unspoken truth is spoken everywhere. God makes a huge dome for the sun—a super dome! The morning sun's a new husband leaping from his honeymoon bed, the

daybreaking sun an athlete racing to the tape. That's how God's Word vaults across the skies from sunrise to sunset, melting ice, scorching deserts, warming hearts to faith. The revelation of God is whole and pulls our lives together."

After studying divine design in Psalm 19, a person would have to be a fool to say that there is no God (Ps 53.1). God exists. God created. He created the world for us because He "chose us in Him before the creation of the world to be holy and blameless in His sight" (Eph 1.4, NIV). Allow this fact to enter your heart: you and I were chosen by Him and in His heart before the foundations of the world were laid. The earth was made for His kids and Christians ought to be leading, by example, in the stewardship of this environment.

The Fact of Conscience

Vine's Expository Dictionary defines the word conscience (Greek suneidesis) as, "a knowing with" (sun, "with," oida, "to know"), as "a co-knowledge (with oneself), the witness borne to one's conduct by conscience, that faculty by which we can apprehend the will of God, as that which is designed to govern our lives." Strong's Concordance says it is "co-perception, moral consciousness." Nelson says it is "a person's inner awareness of his conforming to the will of God or his departing from it, and resulting in a sense of approval or a sense of condemnation."

Life Purpose

All men and women, everywhere, share a common moral sense of right and wrong. This has resulted in a commonly held and respected system of laws, responsibility, and accountability. Romans 1.19 makes it very clear to us: "What is known about God is evident to mankind and made plain in their inner consciousness [conscience]." Everyone, everywhere, instinctively knows the difference between right or wrong.

> ***People instinctively know the difference between right or wrong.***

The laws we make reflect our internal belief system. The Apostle Paul states in Romans 2.14-16 (NIV):

> "(Indeed, when Gentiles, who do not have the law, do by nature things required by the law, they are a law unto themselves, even though they do not have the law, since they show that the requirements of the law are written on their hearts, their consciences also bearing witness, and their thoughts now accusing, now even defending them.) This will take place on the day when God will judge men's secrets."

The mere fact that everyone shares a common conscience, both multi-generationally and cross-culturally, should cause us to think about a Creator. Since we all feel that we will be held accountable for our actions, whether we reject, neglect, or honor our conscience helps us to consider the consequences of our actions.

As Christians, we believe that moral absolutes come to us through a Creator who established moral laws in the universe. To submit to the revealed moral law of God [the Bible] is to know peace in the heart and order in society. To reject it is to know confusion in the heart and chaos in society. Man cannot dismiss God (Gal 6.6-9) and break His laws with impunity: there will be consequences.

To sin is to *"miss the mark."* When man sins, he misses the mark of God's intentions, degrades himself, and begins to fall apart. Read through the creation and fall account in Genesis 2 and 3. There was a law maker; a law; a knowing of right and wrong; a sense of conscience; accountability; and a Judge. The very same principle applies to communities and nations. When cities sin, they rot from the inside out.

Repentance and personal transformation occurs when people are drawn back into a relationship with God and His ways. Revival and social transformation occurs when a city or country is being reconciled to God's ways. That is the only thing that will cause a nation and its people to prosper.

The Face of Christ

The *act of creation* and the *fact of conscience* lead us to the *face of Christ*. God sent His Son so that we could know Him and by knowing Him, love Him, as He has loved us. Christ is not just an historical figure:

Life Purpose

He is God in the flesh—to know Him is to know God himself. To hear Him speak and to see Him act is to come to know ourselves. Purpose starts with relationship.

C. S. Lewis made this comment:

> "The more we get out of the way and let Him take us over, the more truly ourselves we become. The more we resist Him and try to live on our own, the more we become dominated by our own hereditary and upbringing and surroundings and natural desires."

A Christian is one who has stopped resisting an intimate relationship with the Creator.

> **We think we are looking for something: we realize we are found by Someone.**

Finally, many years ago Augustine penned in Book One of *Confessions:* "You have made us for yourself, and our hearts are restless until they find their rest in You." All of us start out searching, but we end up being discovered. We think we are looking for something: we realize we are found by Someone. We have recognized the fact that we can't locate God unless God himself initiates it! If the chasm between Creator and His creation is to be bridged, God must build it! And He did, in Jesus Christ!

> **It is impossible for you to stay where you are and go on with God.**

Chapter 4
Solomon: A Post-Modern Man?

"The tragedy of life is not that it ends so soon, but that we wait so long to begin it."
Anonymous

> Someone asked a concert violinist
> in New York's Carnegie Hall
> how she became so skilled. She said
> it was by "planned neglect."
> She planned to neglect everything
> that was not related to her goal.
>
> *Illustrations for Biblical Preaching* (page 101)

Solomon is a perfect illustration of someone who knew his life purpose and then lost his way. The writer of the wonderful book of wisdom, Proverbs, is also the same man who penned the tragedy called Ecclesiastes. It is my observation that Solomon started his journey in life, on track, and then veered off course. That led to a downward spiral from which we do not know if he ever recovered.

What happened to Solomon? What pulled him off track and caused him to run a different race? Rollo May stated: *"It is an old and ironic habit of human beings to run faster when we have lost our way!"* There are a lot of people who are going faster but are getting nowhere: their bumper stickers should read, *"Don't follow me—I'm lost."*

> **"It is an old and ironic habit of human beings to run faster when we have lost our way!"**
> Rollo May

I do not want my life to imitate Solomon's spiritual and moral decline until he despaired of life itself! I want my life to count, to be filled with purpose until my dying day. I want to complete my course in faith, persevering until the end in the very specific thing God has required of me.

Let's take a look at Solomon's life because it brings us some very key lessons.

Solomon's Background

Solomon was the second beloved son of Bathsheba and David, born around the middle 900s B.C. His alternate name was Jedediah, meaning *"beloved of the Lord."* He reigned over Israel 40 years (970–930 B.C.).

During his early reign, Solomon demonstrated such incredible wisdom. He divided the entire country into twelve major districts, each taxed for one month to take care of the King's court; he constructed the temple in a record seven years [note: it took Solomon thirteen years to build his own house] and in doing this, Solomon demonstrated he placed God first; he established a system of trade with the nations around him, land and sea, and prospered like no other king of his day; and he wrote 3000 parables and 1005 songs (1Ki 4.32; 11.41) and many influential people came to hear him speak, such as the Queen of Sheba (1Ki 10).

Solomon's Call

Read through 1 Chronicles 28.2-20 and you will no doubt ascertain that Solomon received a number of prophetic words from his father, King David, shortly before the elder statesman went on to be with the Lord.

In essence, King David told Solomon that God had chosen him to build a house for the presence of the Lord. And, as long as Solomon placed God first, He would establish Solomon as king over Israel. All Solomon had to do was know the God of his father and obey His commandments and ordinance.

The Blessing of Obedience to The Purpose

Solomon is appointed king as his father had prophetically stated (1Ch 29.22). The Lord was with him, strengthened his kingdom, and made him exceedingly great (2Ch 1.1).

Life Purpose

When the Lord said to Solomon, *"Ask what I shall give to you"* (verse 7), Solomon very wisely chose wisdom instead of wealth, possessions, honour, the life of his enemies, or even long life.

Because Solomon acted unselfishly, he received wisdom plus the above, being made a king without equal (verses 8-12). He completed building the temple with plans, people, and a seasonal life purpose; then God filled the house with His glory (2Ch 5.11-14; 7.1-3). He led a united nation with leaders who were subject to, and willing, to heed his directives; and, finally, God affirmed His covenantal promise to Solomon if he walked uprightly before Him.

Why did I go over these scriptures? To help you see that Solomon's life began with divine purpose. As long as he was pursuing God's purpose for his life, all things worked together for his good. When Solomon moved away from seeking God's purpose, his life began to fall apart and devolution occurred.

"Whatever my eyes desired, I kept not from them. I withheld not my heart from any pleasure."

Solomon's Demise

1 Kings 11.1-14 is an account of Solomon's sorrowful departure from a God-given life purpose into a self-indulgent lifestyle and, consequently, downward spiral, the familiar kind that he speaks to us about in Ecclesiastes 2: "have a good time . . . cheer

my body with wine . . . build myself up and become great . . . whatever my eyes desired I kept not from them; I withheld not my heart from any pleasure."

Where did his downward spiral begin? Where it does with all of us: Romans 1.21 states that "when we knew Him as God, we failed to honour Him as God or give Him thanks." God adamantly told Solomon, "No compromise!" Yet, "Solomon defiantly loved many foreign women" (1Ki 11.1) which clearly contradicted God's purpose for his life and destiny (verse 2).

Scripture implies that these things became his purpose for life and they "turned his heart away from God" (verse 3). It was not long before, in his old age, "his heart was turned after other gods" (verse 4). He built them temples and altars to sacrifice upon. "And the Lord was very angry . . . and stirred up an adversary against Solomon" (verses 9, 14).

We read about Solomon's spiritual and mental state in Ecclesiastes 1. He came to see all of his activities as purposeless. He saw his life as temporal, being lived out "under the sun" (1.3) as contrasted to living his life under or in the Son.

What were his proofs or logic for this conclusion? Well, he points to nature's monotony. No matter what happens, the earth remains the same (verses 1-7)—the generations, sun, wind, rivers, and so on. All of nature sadly reminds him of his own experience with boredom and repetition: the schedules, cycles, timetables—for instance, the sea is never filled or the streams ever emptied.

He makes the point that human life is also

Life Purpose

monotonous: there's never enough, there's absolutely nothing new (verses 8-11)—everything is wearisome, full of labour and work, more than one can say—the eye, the ear, what has been will be, what has been done will be done. No one remembers the old or what they've done, and that cycle is never going to change! Solomon's life at this point surely indicates someone on a downward spiral.

What is Solomon saying?

- There is really no gain to life.
- There is never anything truly new under the sun.
- No one will remember me for what I've done.

Solomon illustrates these personal realities by what he says in verses 12-18. He hasn't just sat around with these miseries! He has studied and explored every source to help him locate wisdom, not unlike the drive of people today in their pursuit of knowledge (2Ti 3.7). He finishes by saying that God has placed a very heavy burden upon men, unlike Christ's statements (Mt 11.28-30) or Peter's (1Pe 5.7).

Still, Solomon can't make any sense whatsoever out of the human condition. He painstakingly asks these questions: "What is my life's purpose, my reason for existence? Why was I born? What am I to do with my life? What's after death? Is this all there is to life?"

"Why was I born? What am I to do with my life?"

When a man who had wisdom, wealth, women, and power asks a question like that, it is definitely worth listening to and carefully evaluating!

Solomon's reflections point to the futile conclusions made by a man living without God—a godless life! His empire had been built, like his life, on the shifting sands of change rather than the rock of his salvation (Mt 7.24-29). His neglect of God's purpose *for* his life opened up the stage for a crisis in his life.

What do we learn from Solomon's debating with life? Everything is meaningless without God—it is what's above the sun that really counts and actions without His direction have little effect on life; a man receives no gain from his labour when it is done for selfish ends (Php 3.8); there is nothing new under the sun, but coming to know the Son makes all things new (2Co 5.17). Man's memory is very short—but God's is everlasting. Man forgets—but God never will (2Co 5.10).

R.C. Sproul appropriately points out in his book *The Hunger for Significance* that "modern man has an aching void. The emptiness we feel cannot be relieved by a new car, a better job, and a bigger house. It can only be filled by understanding that each human life is far from meaningless" (cover).

If who you are and what you are doing does not satisfy or give you a sense of life significance, then you need to make a change. If you keep doing what you have always done, your future is going to remain unchanged and unchallenged. If your destiny is going to change, it will require changes now.

Life Purpose

Make a decision to come to your Creator—who created you for purpose—and seek out His intention and will for your life. There is no more living your life within the cage of quiet desperation. No more struggling to find a reason for existence. No more living each day as an exercise in futility and vanity. Only a creationist view can open the door for significance and living your life with a personal purpose.

Listen to and live out some godly wisdom: "He has made everything beautiful in its time; He also has planted eternity in men's heart *and* mind [a divinely implanted sense of a purpose working through the ages which nothing under the sun, but God alone, can satisfy]" (Eccl 3.11, AMP).

I want to state to you unequivocally that *"your life is far from meaningless"* because etched into each individual is a life purpose, like Solomon's, with God-established plans and intentions. Each and every person alive today has the same potential for success or failure that Solomon experienced. The choice is yours!

> **"Start with the end in mind."**
> Stephen Covey

Chapter 5

An Identity Crisis

"Those who quit their proper character to assume what does not belong to them are, for the greatest part, ignorant of both the character they leave and of the character they assume."

Edmund Burke

"Our chief want in life is somebody who shall make us what we can be."

Ralph Waldo Emerson

"And so I insist—and God backs me up on this—that there be no going along with the crowd, the empty-headed, mindless crowd. They've refused for so long to deal with God that they've lost touch not only with God but with reality itself. They can't think straight anymore . . . Since, then, we do not have the excuse of ignorance, everything connected with that old way of life has to go. It's rotten through and through. Get rid of it! And then take on an entirely new way of life—a God-fashioned life, a life renewed from the inside and

Life Purpose

working itself into your conduct as God accurately reproduces His character in you. What this adds up to, then, is this: no more lies, no more pretense."

Ephesians 4.17-25, *The Message Translation*

This purposeless generation is founded upon *five* fundamental belief systems that have governed our social thinking for years. These belief systems have shaped and continue to shape a world that finds itself in an identity crisis.

The first belief system is *Secular Humanism:* man is at the center of the universe, not God, and man is the arbiter of all truth. Man may have caused some of his problems; however, he does have the ability to solve them his own way. There are no absolutes. If man needs to change the rules, he can do that. *"There is no God—just man!"* This statement leads us to the conclusion that man is alone with himself, by himself. What a thought! Then you start to wonder and ponder these questions: What am I doing in this universe? Why am I here? Where am I going? Who cares? And, worst of all, who is there left to blame?"

> **"The first thing you need to know is that you are an accident."**
> Frank Peretti

The second belief system is *Evolution:* man is evolving, and yet, he appears to be devolving. The first science class builds that thought into the younger generation.

Frank Peretti's take on what the teacher may have said that very first day is comical, because it is too close to reality. He calls it *"goo to you by the way of the zoo."*

"First and foremost, before we learn anything, the first thing you need to know is that you are an accident. You are a totally meaningless conglomeration of molecules that came together purely by chance millions and billions of years ago. Dust and gas of the universe sort of floated around and bumped into each other and finally said, *"I know. Let's create man!"*
Then they became organic and created a primordial soup, grew flippers and fins, grew legs and crawled up on the land and sort of started growing fur and feathers, and eating bugs and other stuff, became bigger, then stood to their feet and became a monkey, an ape. Then the ape decided to shave and he became an evolutionist."

By adopting that scientific view of their humanity, it is very little wonder why this generation has such a frightening view of life. This generation escaped the pill, beat abortion, and survived. However, survival isn't living! It's existing!

The very body they live in has been dehumanized. The baby is no longer viewed as a child in the womb, but as an unnecessary appendage, an unwanted child, a tumor to be aborted. The aged are no longer desirable and are looked upon as nothing more than a

Life Purpose

drain on our resources, sadly left to face an uncertain future in a culture contemplating euthanasia as a final solution. What in the world have we come to? The body that God created has lost its human dignity. Instead of consecrating the body for God's use, the body has been pierced, painted, tattooed, and finally, cremated. When one rejects a Creator, then one despises the creation! Instead of speaking of human body parts with dignity, the body has been degraded with a new vocabulary.

Psychology is the third belief system: we now have to create a way of dealing with the problems we have made by rejecting the existence of God. Psychology says, *"You are an accident, but you are a good accident: we need to help you feel really good about yourselves!"* Just think of the incredible potential you have for creating a multitude of other good accidents.

Freudian psychology maintains that man is evil. Rogerian psychology emphasizes that man is good. Lastly, Skinnerian psychology says that man is neither—he is a zipher! That sort of clears everything up—take your pick.

Our society is in utter confusion as to who they really are, how to fix themselves and make themselves whole. Outside of a personal experience with our heavenly Father and a welcome of holiness, people will never find the wholeness it seeks. That comes from God alone.

> **We are all gods: we just forgot that we were!**

The fourth belief system that leads to an identity crisis is *New Age Cultism:* this is when any aspect of psychology cannot answer a questioning heart and the God shaped vacuum remains. Because of this dilemma we see modern pilgrimages into other cultures and religions: for example, The Beatles and their pursuit of the Maharishi and Transcendental Meditation.

Other searches include taking a variety of motivational courses at our workplace, researching our hidden potential. We use only ten percent of our brain anyway, and if we can tap into that other ninety percent, there is nothing we cannot do. The philosophy behind these motivational courses is whatever man can conceive, he can achieve. Any limitations that exist in our life are only in the mind. Once we master the mind, we are quickly moving on our way to the top.

Where has that kind of thinking led us? To a belief system that says men are not sinners: the idea of sin is a concoction of organized religion to manipulate and control people. Our problem is not moral trespass; it is just ignorance. We are all gods: we just forgot that we were (that's some kind of god that forgets that he is god: what good is that going to do you if you remember just to forget again?).

New Agers advocate that there is divine potential in every one of us. We merely have to discover our higher selves, achieve enlightenment, attain our own godhood, gain self-realization: get into the crystals, the tarot cards, meditation. We need to find ourselves and others from beyond (channel the spirits). Why? To gain power to manipulate reality, to control people's lives, to be God over other people. This, of course, opens the doors to spirit guides until a generation is in such spiritual bondage, they cannot escape. They have met their maker and it is not the true God, but the god of this world or the god of their own making (2Co 4.4).

The last belief system is *Satanism:* this is a strong belief in the supernatural realm outside of God. Turn on the television set and look at the numbers of people who are desperately desiring spiritual help from astrologers. Take a trip to your local bookstore and see the variety of books that are available on the very same subject. Witchcraft and Wicca have been repackaged for sale to a new generation. What newspaper could do without a horoscope (or, a horror scope)? Satanism is the spirit of anti-Christ: its main intention is not as much an opposing of Christ as it is a displacing and replacing Christ with its own doctrine of life.

Is it any wonder that this generation has emerged with such an identity crisis? Identity implies identification. We take our identity from what we identify with. When we came from no one or nothing, what does that do to our sense of identity? It leads to a crisis. If we came from no one or nothing and are going nowhere, what does that say about our own sense of value and significance, as well as our sense of personal destiny?

If our Creator is not in the equation of life, our need for self-esteem will be corrupted by pride—

comparing ourselves to others or competing with others for recognition; the quest for material provision will degenerate into covetousness; the hunger for personal intimacy will diminish into endless lustful associations; the drive to succeed will plummet into apathy and indifference; the search to receive honor and affirmation will be contaminated by envy and jealousy; and the desire to be accepted and affirmed will be polluted with selfish agendas and manipulated praise.

> **When we came from no one or nothing, that leads to a crisis.**

The Search for Value

If your sense of identity is not found in God as Creator, then your sense of value and esteem must be found in something else. This crossless generation is being forced to find their sense of esteem from society around them, and that is usually formed by the majority's influence. The majority of people identifies what it takes to take on value.

Dr. James Dobson wrote a book called Hide or Seek and in it he described three areas where humanity is left seeking to find their place of significance and value. If we, as believers, are not careful, we will also be pulled into the dragnet of this deceptive, powerful force in society and end up building our sense of who

Life Purpose

we are (identity) and personal esteem (value) around these three self-defeating equations.

1. Personal attractiveness—outward appearance, youth or age, physical beauty or ugliness—how you appear to others (your image);
2. Personal intelligence—scholastic achievement, degrees and institutional associations, educational merit, job position—what you can do or what you know; and
3. Personal material worth—sound financial security, social status—what you can buy or what you are worth. What you acquire is never enough.

Without a belief in the Creator God, man is left to create for himself a value system that gives him a sense of significance and worth. It is built upon differentiation, comparison, and competition as compared to the uniqueness of the individual and aiding in their personal development and advancement.

Let's look at these three equations more thoroughly.

#1 Appearance + Affection = Significance, Personal Worth, and Value

Studies have shown that people have a tendency to respond differently to an unusually beautiful

46

child than to a homely child, and that difference has a profound impact upon that child's developing personality, vision of him or herself, and their personal destiny.

As George Orwell said: *"All [people] are created equal, but some are more equal than others."* Children begin to sense that unequal treatment very early in life (such as the emergence of a beauty cult). Teachers tend to distrust and mark differently the answers of the uglier child and then discipline them more firmly. Kids pick up on this.

This thinking even invades traditional children's stories: some good examples are The Ugly Duckling; Sleeping Beauty; Rudolph the Red-Nosed Reindeer; Dumbo the Elephant; Snow White and the Seven Dwarfs; and Cinderella. By the time the kids reach kindergarten, many have already determined their relative worth by comparison. They can easily and quickly pick apart each other's differences, deformities, and lacks: such as nicknames. Each of us can relate to the above scenario.

By the time the child becomes a teenager, their physical attractiveness has become extremely significant. By the time the teenager becomes an adult and the body begins to sag, wrinkle, and droop after many diets, plastic surgery, new fads and daily workouts, time has erased the advantage of firm shapely bodies and youthful skin.

It is really critical we remember that the outward appearance is just the frame for the real thing. You know there is a *downside* to this way of thinking:

Firstly, it leads to a belief in the accruing value of

a person based upon beauty and age, rather than an understanding of inherent value regardless of beauty or age;

> *"All [people] are created equal, but some are more equal than others."*
> George Orwell

Secondly, it creates a lifestyle that perpetuates a beauty that is skin deep and immensely costly to maintain—for example, billion dollar industries service the drive to stay young and beautiful, and usually, working; and

Thirdly, we will all still get old and lose our young looks. Then what will become of our sense of personal worth and meaningful significance?

Looking the best that you can is a very positive trait, but God values something much deeper than the shiny skin and quality clothing. He is looking upon the heart (1Sa 16.7). Man does look upon the outward appearance, so do your best to present yourself in the best way possible. Remember, though, it doesn't matter about other people's respect or estimation of your worth. There is One who looks at you far differently: God, your Heavenly Father. His evaluation of the heart is more important in determining your worth than that of any person.

The following illustration is an excellent example of what I am trying to convey to you.

A well-known speaker started off his seminar by holding up a $20 bill. He asked his audience, "Who would like this $20 bill?" Hands shot up all over the room. He said, "I am going to give this $20 bill to one of you but first let me do this." He then proceeded to crumple the money. He then asked, "Who still wants it?" Still the hands shot up. "Well," he replied, "what if I do this?" He dropped the paper bill on the ground and started to grind it into the floor with his shoe. The money was now wrinkled and dirty. "Now who still wants it?" The people still continued to raise their hands.

"My friends," he quietly stated, "you have all learned a very valuable lesson. No matter what I did to the money you all still wanted it, because it did not decrease in value. It was still worth $20. Many times in our lives we are dropped, crumpled, and ground into the dirt by decisions we make, by loved ones, and also by the myriad of circumstances that come our way. We feel we are worthless. But no matter what has happened or what will happen to you, you will never lose your value—dirty or clean, crumpled or finely creased, you are still priceless to those who love you. The worth of our lives comes not in what we do, or who we know, but by who we are. You are special and don't ever forget it."

#2 Performance + Affection = Significance, Personal Worth, and Value

Simply put: intelligence has become an extremely critical attribute in evaluating the worth of a person in

Life Purpose

this generation. *In her book The Child Worshippers* Martha Weinman Lear makes the observation that the younger generation is really the status symbol of the previous (parents): for instance, their kids must be very gifted, talented, and excel above all else. Education becomes the god a generation serves and many pay the price to achieve it.

The impact of ignorance is quick, leading a child to sense his or her own relative stupidity: we hear of killer terms like the slow learner, the semi-literate, the underachiever, the late bloomer, or the culturally deprived. Many children become destined to a lifetime of challenges because of this sense of slow-wittedness that they now believe cannot ever be changed about themselves. Can you relate to that?

Here are some things that are worth considering. We are all ignorant, only in different ways and areas. Knowledge is increasing so incredibly fast that even those who specialize in certain fields of expertise are being left behind by new information and technology: no one is indispensable—how long before a bachelor's degree has become outdated? What you knew ten years ago makes you and your job obsolete and replaceable today.

> **The worth of our lives comes not in what we do or who we know, but by who we are.**

Knowledge, in itself, does not satisfy the hunger in a man's heart to know God, to know himself, and to know his purpose. You can have knowledge, but without an intimacy with God there will be a lack of wisdom to live. We all know that there is a huge difference between making a living and making a life.

#3 Status + Affection = Significance, Personal Worth, and Value

Every one of us knows the effect money or the lack thereof can have upon people, their ultimate friendships, character, and influence in life. "A friend who isn't in need is a friend indeed!"

"Wealth makes friends [acquaintances]" (Pr 19.4). "If you have the money, honey, I have the time!"

Money brings the ability to purchase recognition. It also brings with it position and influence. But, just like the Rich Young Ruler in Luke 18 when Jesus attempted to separate him from his security blanket by asking him to release his finances, many people find out how really insecure and worthless they feel without the image of being rich and influential.

No matter what your financial situation looks like, you know there is a *downside* to an individual placing his or her trust in this kind of value system.

Money comes and goes—mostly goes: if one does not have character, money will be wasted and end up doing little of value; money cannot buy very much that is temporarily or eternally valuable; there will always be those who have more money or less money

Life Purpose

than you do (one scenario would lead to less personal significance; the other to pride). Unless you see money as a divinely given resource with supernatural responsibility, the best you can do is build bigger barns and leave it to a generation that will not value it, but waste it. Look where this value system got the Prodigal Son in Luke 15. When he had wealth, everyone was his friend; when he became penniless, he was left alone to fend for himself in a pig pen. True friends "love at all times" (Pr 17.17).

Where Do We Get Our Identity and Value?

I love the ocean and have been blessed to live on both Canadian coastlines, Nova Scotia and British Columbia. It is amazing to see the tree growth next to windy coastlines. Some trees are very short and stubby, their roots penetrating rock and extremely shallow soil conditions. Some are tall and majestic, their roots two to three times deeper than they are tall. What a magnificent sight!

In both cases, the deeper the root system, the stronger the tree became. Adverse weather conditions seemed only to serve them and cause them to go deeper and grow stronger; thus enabling them to survive the storms of life.

That is what God wants us to do: He wants us to get deeply planted and rooted into who He is. The deeper our spiritual rootage in Him, the stronger our spiritual experience will become. The winds and waves will not move us.

> **If you have the money, honey, I have the time.**

Identity is found in who or what you identify with. The Christian finds his whole identity and worth in his relationship with God. It is God who created you and set the value or worth of your soul. Jesus Christ said, "For what shall it profit a man, if he shall gain the whole world, and lose his own soul?" (Mk 8.36, KJV). The worth of your life is equated to the whole world. Believe it, because it's the truth!

Look at this illustration. A middle-aged business executive approached the front entrance of the office building in which he worked. A young feminist came up at the same moment, so he stepped back and held the door open for her to pass on through. She looked at him and said with annoyance, "Don't hold the door open for me just because I'm a lady."

To her surprise, he looked right back at her and replied, "I'm not. I'm holding it open because I'm a gentleman."

Likewise, we as Christians must always act toward others on the basis of what we are in Christ, and not on the basis of what they may or may not be *(Illustrations for Biblical Preaching,* page 38).

The value of something is very often determined by what a person will give in exchange for it. A

Life Purpose

painting's value is never determined or insured until someone puts a purchase price on it. When it came to your life, God saw such value in you that He gave His Son's life as a divine exchange for your life.

God put everything on the line for you. He created you and loves you! He paid for your life with His precious blood. You no longer belong to yourself, but to Him. Therefore, when making statements like:

- I can't!
- I haven't got the qualifications or abilities!
- No one likes me!
- Why should anyone listen to me!
- I haven't got any money!
- No one knows who I am!
- Send someone else to do it!
- I haven't got what it takes!

—you undermine God's ability to direct you along a path towards your role in bringing about His purpose in your life. These kinds of phrases grieve your heavenly Father. God knows you better than you know yourself—He created you for a purpose and gave you value. Therefore, it is critical that you start to see yourself through His eyes and stop believing what others have told you, or what you have told yourself about you.

If He spoke to you right now, could you listen? Do you have principles ingrained into your spiritual life that will enable you to listen to the voice of God, hear it with your head, believe it with your heart, and act on it in faith? If not, what God is capable of doing, and wants to do through you, is very limited by a limited and inaccurate belief system that needs to be overcome (2Co 10.3-5).

> **The value of something is often determined by what someone will give for it.**

The Christian Magna Carta

When you are discouraged, believing that God cannot use you, think carefully of the following principles based on the Christian Magna Carta.

"God loves you with an everlasting love" (Jer 31.3). He knows aspects about your life that no one will ever know, and He still loves you.

"Your life is genuinely special." In Exodus 19.5, He calls you "His special possession." Deuteronomy 32.10 states,"You are the apple of His eye."

"Though fully known, you are fully accepted" (Ro 15.7). God has you tattooed in the palm of His hand (Isa 49.16).

"You are in process—His plan is in process" (Php 1.6). He is the potter and you are the clay. "Be patient; God is not finished with you yet!" You are a Christian and you are becoming Christian on a daily basis. You are His workmanship and His poetry, still being worked on, still being written upon that your life may

Life Purpose

serve as a book to be read of all people, everywhere. If you still need convincing that God wants to use you, read on—because Ephesians 1 says that God:

"Chose us." You are not here by chance. You are here by His choice. You were in His heart before He created the world. As a matter of fact, the world was created with you, specifically, in mind, to be ruled over by you. Isn't that awesome?

"Predestined us." His eternal intention was your adoption into the family. He was not forced to consider this: it was His pleasure and will.

"Redeemed us." He redeemed your life from sin and its degradation. He took you from slavery into freedom, from guilt and condemnation into forgiveness.

"The mystery of His will is made known to us." You were never meant to live your life in confusion. He intended you to be in the know about what He is doing so that you could serve His purpose in your generation.

Always remember: when God created the world, He spoke it into being (Heb 1.3). When God created man, He formed him with His own hands and breathed life into him with His own breath. How absolutely incredible to know that each one of us is personally hand-made and Spirit-breathed.

> ***Once you see your identity,***
> ***you will see your assignment.***

Chapter 6
A Father's Heart

When John F. Kennedy was president of the UnitedStates, security was frequently tight. But one picture captivated the hearts of the American people as his littleson, affectionately called John-John, sneaked by allthe security personnel and curled up close to his daddy.He had instant access. It didn't matter what any of the secret-service agents said, John-John could comeany time he wanted to because he was the son.

Charles Stanley, *The Glorious Journey* (page 186)

The Father's Love Letter
Barry Adams (1999)

God loves you. He is the Father you have been looking for all your life. This is His love letter to you.

My child, you may not know Me, but I know you—Ps 139.1
I know when you sit down and when you rise up—Ps 139.2
For you have been made in My image—Ge 1.26-27
I knew you even before you were conceived—Jer 1.4-5
You are not a mistake—Ps 139.15-16
I determined the exact time of your birth and where you would live

Life Purpose

I have been misrepresented by those who do not know Me—Jn 8.41-44
I offer you more than your earthly father ever could—Mt 7.11
I am the perfect Father—Mt 5.48
For I am your provider and meet your needs—Mt 6.31-33
My plan for your future has always been filled with hope—Jer 29.11
I rejoice over you with singing—Zep 3.17
I will never stop doing good to you—Jer 32.40
You are My treasured possession—Ex 19.5
I want to show you great and marvelous things—Jer 33.3
If you will seek Me with all your heart, you will find Me—Dt 4.29
Delight in Me and I will give you the desires of your heart—Ps 37.4
I am able to do more for you than you can possibly imagine—Eph 3.20
For I am your greatest encourager—2Th 2.16-17
I am also the Father who comforts you in all your troubles—2Co 1.3-4
When you are broken-hearted, I am close to you—Ps 34.18
One day I will wipe away every tear from your eyes—Rev 21.3-4
And I will take away all the pain you have suffered—Rev 21.3-4
I gave up everything that I might gain your love—Ro 8.31-32
If you receive the gift of My Son, Jesus, you receive Me—1Jn 2.23
Nothing will ever separate you from My love again—Ro 8.39
Come home and I will throw the biggest party ever seen—Lk 15.7
I have always been Father and I will always be Father—Eph 3.14-15
My question is, "Will you be My child?"—Jn 1.12-13
I am waiting for you—Lk 15.11-32

Your Dad, Almighty God

God is no absentee father. He is not dead as the secular humanists and evolutionists would want you to believe. Gary Smalley and John Trent made this statement in the book they co-authored called The Blessing: "No matter your age, the approval of your parents affects how you view yourself and your ability to pass that approval along to your children, spouse, and friends. Many people spend a lifetime looking for this acceptance that the Bible calls *'the blessing'"* (the cover).

This generation has been robbed of a parental relationship with their Heavenly Father and so, the blessing; however, they still try to find it from every possible source. We see an incredible biblical illustration of that in the life of Jacob.

Jacob initially attempted to obtain the blessing from his father through deception (Ge 27.30); then he endeavoured to get God's blessing by *cutting a deal* (Ge 28.20); and finally, he sought to get the blessing from his Uncle Laban by working diligently in the family's business (Ge 31.1-2).

> ***Many people spend a lifetime looking for this acceptance the Bible calls 'the blessing.***

None of this settled the issue. Jacob found himself running away from Laban to facing his brother Esau, whom he had underhandedly robbed of his birthright and his blessing. Despite doing this, he still did not feel blessed. Genesis 32 states he was "left alone [at the brook called Jabbok]." It was at Jabbok that Jacob had to deal with himself, his nature, and his actions that had separated him from his destiny. It was at Jabbok that Jacob would experience one of those life-changing moments that transformed his destiny.

He cried out as he wrestled with the Angel, "I will not let You go, except You bless me" (Ge 32.26

Life Purpose

NIV). In that God encounter, Jacob experienced a nature change and a name change. His divine destiny commenced from that moment of knowing God and knowing himself. He got the birthright, the blessing, and the benediction at the same time. His life was truly transformed. He realized true blessing does not happen apart from a personal relationship to His Heavenly Father.

No one can get the blessing through deceitfulness or through trickery, deal making, or even through diligence. It comes through an honouring relationship. It comes when you have acknowledged your need to have the essential questions of life answered, so that life takes on meaning and purpose.

Our Heavenly Father desires to impart that blessing to every individual, in every generation, irrespective of tongue or colour. However, a generation must desire it, not despise it. God will not reveal Himself or His purpose to a generation that does not acknowledge His existence. He says in Hebrews 11.6: "And without faith it is impossible to please God, because anyone who comes to Him must believe that He exists and that He rewards those who earnestly seek Him"(NIV).

Jacob sought this blessing from his father as a desperate man seeks out water in a thirsty land. Unfortunately, Esau, his brother, only pined for it: *"Have you only one blessing, my father? Bless me, even me also, O my father"* (Ge 27.34)—he did not desperately seek it out. He eventually wound up despising something he did not get.

This blessing, or lack of it, affects your ability to hear the voice and heart of Father God when He wants to open up His heart to you and prepare you for your life purpose. Scripture makes it clear that Jesus himself gained a sense of personal worth and value from the blessing He received from His Father (His baptism, Mt 3.17).

It is very important to note that His Father's affirmation—"This is My beloved Son, in whom I am well pleased"—was not based upon what Jesus had done, because He had not begun His ministry. He had not done any mighty works or deeds. He had spent most of His life getting to know His Father (the first 30 years). The Heavenly Father's affirmation was based entirely upon who Jesus was and not on what works He had accomplished.

The Father's purpose was constantly at the forefront of Christ's thinking. Jesus made this statement in Luke 2.49: "I must be in My Father's house and occupied with My Father's business." He says in John 3.8, "For this purpose was the Son of God made manifest, to destroy the works of the evil one." And, in John 16.28, Jesus talks about the Father's continuous direction.

> **Our parenting had a profound impact on our own sense of identity, purpose, and destiny.**

The Father's Blessing

We can all identify with the fact that our parenting had quite a profound impact on our own sense of identity, purpose, and destiny. In particular, our natural earthly fathers had an extremely significant influence in the way we developed a sense of personal value and upon how we responded to the many challenges of life—either confidently, or insecurely. A lot of people regard God the Father in the same manner as their earthly father.

All good, natural fathers influence their children with godly affection (Mk 10.13-16); verbally affirm them with words of grace (Eph 4.29), knowing that the tongue sets on fire the course of their life (Jas 3.5-6, NASB); prophetically confirm to them things in their spirit, as Isaac confirmed his son Jacob's identity and destiny (Ge 27.27-29); and continually challenge them to be their best.

A Father Movement

As a young adult, I had the privilege of witnessing and also being a participant in the *Jesus Movement* and the *Charismatic Movement*. Today, the Church has entered another movement we will prophetically call the *Father Movement*. There are clear signs that a revelation of the Father is in the Father's response to a fatherless generation. We see evidence this movement is gaining tremendous momentum. Many are writing about it because it has some very unique characteristics.

The prodigals are being called back into a relationship with God and His Church; a last day's ministry to all family systems is touching the heart of men (such as the Promise Keepers), making the whole family strong and active for God; worship songs are being spoken from the Father Heart of God to His Church and are being expressed back to Him (Jn 4.23-24); there is a new and unique governmental formulation and networking of apostolic ministries (Heb 12); and, lastly, there is a positioning and commissioning of men and women and ministries (called *the blessing*).

All of these emphases point to one thing: the emergence of a fresh, new revelation of the Father Heart of God. It is this personal relationship to the Father that is absolutely critical for developing our personal security and confidence, for that will help us respond obediently to His voice and our life purpose.

A Father's Spiritual Inheritance

Every natural father has an inheritance and legacy to deposit into the lives of his children. The *Heavenly Father*, like the earthly father, also has something very precious to give away to this generation.

Life Purpose

He imparts to every one of His kids a sense of identity (Ro 8.14-16). *Note:* Many of God's children are still acting as slaves and not heirs of Jesus Christ. As long as unworthiness locks up the heart they will constantly be locked into a performance mentality, and they will never be able to enter the joys of sonship and also enjoy the benefits of their natural inheritance.

The Father Movement.

He provides protection and provision for you. This is entirely based upon our relationship: "If God be for us, who can be against us?" (Ro 8.31).

He trains and disciplines you as a son and daughter of the King (Heb 12). Do not walk in the dark, as the blind leading the blind, but as a child of the day upon whom the light of God has shone (Eph 5).

You acquire an inheritance from Him (Dt 28) because you are an heir of God and bona-fide joint-heir with Jesus Christ who Himself received the birthright blessing from His Father as the first-born!

He gives you prophetic vision by continually affirming the Word of God to your spirit, giving you divine direction.

Psalm 139

Before you proceed any further, take a walk with me through Psalm 139 and listen intently to God's heart for you and your life purpose.

- He knows you more than you know yourself.
- He understands your thoughts, even those you wouldn't want anyone else to know.
- He searches out your path, evaluating your direction.
- He is acquainted with your ways—He knows quiteintimately all of your habits, likes and dislikes, priorities and dispositions.
- He knows your words before you speak them, and He can help you deal with them before they create a problem for you.
- He has you in the center of His attention.
- He has His hand upon you to lead you, just like a dad does with a child. He is a good Father, and He wants to give you good things.
- He formed you in the womb just the way He intended. You are not an accident and definitely not a mistake.
- There was nothing that was hidden from Him when He formed you.
- He has written a Book about you before you ever breathed one breath, where every day was noted before one day took shape.
- He is constantly thinking about you—if a computer can think of every person in the world six times a second, don't you think God can think of you as much as that or even more?

> ***"God loves each of us as if there were only one of us."***
> Augustine

Life Purpose

Chapter 7

You've Been On My Mind

"Thank you, Lord, for thinking about me."
Mimi McQue

"He has also set eternity inthe hearts of men; yet they cannot fathom what God has done from beginning to end."

Ecclesiastes 3.11, *New International Version*

    I believe that all of us have an ache in our spirit to know God's purpose and intention for our lives. I also believe that God is more willing to reveal His purpose than we are willing to receive it. After many years of pastoring I have found the core problem with many of God's people is not that they do not know His plans and purpose for their life, but they are unwilling to be obedient and pay the price to fulfill it. In other words, it is not a matter of ignorance but obedience or even arrogance.
    However, I really believe that ignorance is not an option or a justification. God will unveil the mystery of His will and make it clear. You can count on that. He is not the author of confusion but the God of order.

What more could we ask for?

I am thoroughly convinced it is easier to know God's will than it is to miss it. We have more working on our behalf to help us be obedient to the "heavenly vision" than we have working against its implementation.

Think about these thoughts for a moment. We have the Holy Spirit to convict and convince us of sin—what is wrong; righteousness—what is right; and judgment—consequence. We have the life of Christ who provides a role-model for us. We have the testimony of the saints who sacrificed their lives to live it truly. We have the written Word of God hidden in our heart to provide motivation and understanding in all our decision making—both easy and difficult. We have preachers of the Word of life who faithfully declare how we ought to live in this world. We have the faithful ministry of conscience to produce the danger signals.

What more could we ask for? As a matter of fact, what we know about the nature and character of God affirms this truth to our heart: God will not judge me guilty of not obeying His will when I did not know what will I was to obey.

The same way earthly fathers train their children on a daily basis, it is also in God's nature (as a father) to teach and train His children so that they know what His will is (Heb 12). He will faithfully outline His will so His children have either one of two responses: obedience or rebellion.

I have been a pastor for almost thirty years now. However, I am not in the ministry. The ministry is in

Life Purpose

me. Wherever I go and whatever I do, the minister goes and does. Each of us is a full-time minister and is in full-time ministry. My role as a leader is to equip the saints to do the work of the ministry, within and also without the Church structure (Eph 4.11-16).

When I speak to people about this, I always get numerous reactions. Some have been taught and believe that only *"called to full-time ministry"* people have the will of God revealed to them. I believe that all of us are called to full-time ministry.

I also encounter many people who do not have confidence that God will hear their prayers for direction and guidance. I sometimes ask them to swear then. They decline. I ask them why? Their response? *"Because God will hear me!"* I find that so tragic: God will hear our swearing and respond with discipline, but He will not hear our cry for direction and respond with clarity. That doesn't make sense to me.

I often ask people if they regularly hear the Holy Spirit convicting them of sin. Most respond they do. That concerns me as well. It tells me that their ears have developed an ability to hear conviction of sin (what is wrong), but their ears are dull to hearing conviction of righteousness (what is right).

This does not accurately describe the Father that I know and love. Confusion is not from God and is not one of the fruits of the Spirit. God wants to talk to us about our future more than we want to know about our future. Almost all of our problems stem from stubborn independence, self-reliance, pride, our personal agendas in life, and our will over God's will. Remember, *we are not here to do our thing* but to do God's will for our lives.

May I add this: the price for knowing God's will is never as high as the cost of doing our own thing. It is much more expensive to disobey than it is to obey.

Each one of us is a full-time minister and is in full-time ministry.

We can rightly assume that God desires man to know Him, and he can, by an act of his will and because of a divine capacity know Him. Scripture is replete with divine bewilderment at the foolishness and arrogance of men who deny God's existence, who neglect to inquire after Him, and refuse Him access into their hearts (Ps 53.1-4; Isa 65.1-3). God asks, "What unrighteousness did your fathers find in Me that they went far from Me?" (Jer 2.5, AMP).

God can be known by you if you desire to know Him (Ac 17.27). However, He requires that you approach Him humbly, acknowledging your spiritual need (Mt 5.6; Isa 66.1-2). If you seek Him, you are given divine assurance that you will find Him (Pr 2.1-8; Lu 11.9-10). When you find Him, He will reveal Himself and share with you His plan for your life purpose.

God knows the beginning from the end. He alone created you. He alone knows for what purpose. Pursuing a relationship with Him is a primary step on the way to discovering your life assignment, who He has called you to be, and what He has called you to do.

Life Purpose

Jeremiah made it clear to Israel, a nation that had rejected God and lost their sense of destiny and purpose, that God had not forsaken them or His good plan for them. Jeremiah 29.11 says: "For I know the thoughts that I think toward you. 'I have not lost sight of My plan for you', just 'for you I have a destiny and a hope'" (Knox).

Though you may have lost sight of God's purpose for your life through discouragement, failure, or disobedience, God has not lost sight of His purpose for you. Return to Him, like Israel did, and He will reconnect you to a life full of significance and destiny. He knows the plans He has for you. They are lodged in His heart.

Ephesians 2.10 says, "For we are God's [own] handiwork (His workmanship), recreated in Christ Jesus, [born anew] that we may do those good works which God predestined (planned beforehand) for us, (taking paths which He prepared ahead of time) that we should walk in them—living the good life which He prearranged and made ready for us to live" (AMP).

The actual Greek word for workmanship gives us our English word, poetry. In a very real way, our lives are His poem. We are His poem that He is writing for the world to read. It is positively critical that when our lives are read by society, they truly bring the Writer of the poem honour and glory.

When God gave the final touch to creation, He started a *"new creation"* (2Co 5.17). That new creation is *you* and *I*. He created the world and rested;

70

however, in creating us, He never sleeps. We are His work, and He is faithfully perfecting that work until it is a finished work.

> **"There is something for you to start that is destined for you to finish."**
> Myles Munroe

Life Purpose

Chapter 8

Getting To Know You

"To accomplish anything definite a man renounces everything else."
George Santayana

"The very credentials these people are waving around as something special, I'm tearing up and throwing out with the trash—along with everything else I used to take credit for. And why? Because of Christ. Yes, all the things I once thought were so important are gone from my life. Compared to the high privilege of knowing Christ Jesus as my Master, firsthand, everything I once thought I had going for me is insignificant—dog dung. I've dumped it all in the trash so that I could embrace Christ and be embraced by him. I didn't want some petty, inferior brand of righteousness that comes from keeping a list of rules when I could get the robust kind that comes from trusting Christ—*God's* righteousness. I gave up all that inferior stuff so I could know Christ personally, experience his resurrection power, be a partner in his suffering, and go all the way with him to death itself. If there was any way to get in on the resurrection from the dead, I wanted to do it. I stay focused on the goal. I'm not saying that I have this all together, that I have it made. But I am well on my way, reaching out for Christ, who has so wondrously reached out for me. Friends, don't get me wrong: by no means do I count myself an expert in all of this, but I've got my eye on the goal, where God is beckoning us onward—to Jesus. I'm off and running, and I'm not turning back."

Philippians 3.7-14, *The Message Translation*

"It's all about Him—it's not about us! History is "His story," not "our story." It is really a high privilege to be given the opportunity to know the God of heaven and to be known intimately by Him. The first priority in life is to get to know God. The second priority is to get to know God. I am sure you get the point.

I have always loved the mission statement of Youth With A Mission, a mission motivated and discipling organization I have had the privilege of serving: *"To know Him and to make Him known."* Before you get a revelation of your life purpose, God will require that you develop a relationship with Him first. Each and every one of us can know God as much as we want to know Him; therefore, the responsibility lies with you to passionately pursue Him."

> **God wants us to pursue relationship before purpose.**

When you want to discover your life purpose, you can do that, because God will intentionally introduce

Himself to you. He wants you to know His Nature; His Attributes; His Character; His Ways and Works; and His Voice and Will.

By getting to know God on these levels, it releases the grace, strength, and confidence to obediently pursue His will. The more intimate, personal knowledge you have of God, the greater the grace or the empowerment to accomplish what He asks you to do. It was this intimacy Jesus had with His Father that enabled Him to confidently fulfill the Father's purpose for His life.

It is absolutely imperative that we get our priorities straight here: God wants us to seek His face before we seek His hand. He wants us to pursue relationship before purpose. That is positively key. Life purpose will flow out of the love that we experience in our relationship with Him. Daniel 11.32 (NAS) declares, "but the people who know their God will display strength and action."

While it is not my purpose to delve too deep theologically, it is critical every Christian know the God they serve. A.W. Tozer emphasized in his timeless book *Knowledge of the Holy:*

> "The gravest question before the Church is always God himself, and the most portentous fact about any man is not what he at any given time may say or do, but what he in his deep heart conceives God to be like. We tend by a secret law of the soul to move toward our mental picture of God (page 9)."

As Tozer declared, it is important that we develop the right mental picture of God. That can only come about by renewing our mind with the Word of God and with daily prayer and supplication. God has revealed Himself through His creation, our conscience, His prophets, and through His Son (Heb 1.1-3). And He left us love letters to read, describing Himself in detail.

Let me summarize what these letters say.

His Nature

God is Spiritual—meaning, His substance is spiritual: Jesus said, "God is Spirit" (Jn 4.24). He is immaterial, without flesh and bones. He is invisible, without form (Dt 4.15-19). "No man has seen God at any time" (Jn 1.18). He is very much alive and well (1Th 1.9), implying that God has emotions, power, and activity. And He is a Person, demonstrating self-consciousness and self-determination.

God is a Spirit. He made you spirit so that you can easily communicate with Him. When an individual loses a physical sense, there is often a compensating that occurs and another sense becomes dominant: for instance, those with blindness often use their smell and hearing to tell them what their eyes used to tell them.

There are some of God's people who live their lives solely by physical and carnal senses. However, God has called us to "walk by faith, and not by sight"

Life Purpose

(2Co 5.7). Learn to develop an ability to "walk in the Spirit" (Gal 5.16) and be "led by the Spirit" (Ro 8.14) to commune with Him.

God is Self-Existent—meaning, God has no origin. He is the "I AM THAT I AM" (Ex 3.14). God cannot be traced to a law of cause as the rest of humanity can be. The prophet Isaiah 43.10 says, "Understand that I am He: before Me there was no God formed, neither shall there be after Me" (KJV). See also Isaiah 44.6-8.

> **"Didn't you guys need me for anything?"**

God is Self-Sufficient—meaning, God possesses everything necessary for complete and utter fulfillment within Himself. Jesus said in John 5.26: "For as the Father has life in Himself, so He has granted the Son to have life in Himself" (NIV). God desires us, but He does not need us: His interest in us emerges strictly from His good pleasure.

Sometimes after a long missions trip away from home, I enter my house to be greeted by "Hi, Dad!" Then after some dialogue I find out that everything went well without me, and that's great! There are times, however, when I have battled with the thought that "no one needs me! They are doing just fine on their own!" Sometimes that thought leaks out and I verbalize, "Didn't you guys need me for anything at all?"

One time the response was really quite priceless. My non co-dependent wife, Carleen, said, "No! I don't need you! I want you, I desire you, I love you,

76

but I don't need you." If only our young people could get a revelation of that statement. It is rooted into the reality that God, the all-sufficient One, indwells us. We are then able to minister to others out of this fullness rather than from a place of depletion.

Let me explain what this means. The natural man has a limited supply of water—for instance, representing all that he is. Humanity consists of two kinds of people: givers and takers. When one gives out of a limited supply, one is soon emptied and has to make a choice. They will continue to be "used," or they will search for someone they can "take" from to replenish their supply.

Everyone watches their water levels. Deals are cut between people every day when there is a perceived win-win situation: for example, *"I will say sorry, if you say you are sorry!"*

Breakdowns very often occur in marriage because of this scenario; one takes, the other gives. One gets tired of giving and feels depleted, one is given into by someone else. Finally, the one who is depleted leaves to take what another is giving to replenish their own supply. This creates an ongoing cycle of depletion and replenishment through giving and taking, using and being used. This destructive behaviour has to stop, and it can stop through a proper understanding of God. He wants us to be continually connected to Him, an inner artesian supply of water that never goes dry.

In John 4.13-15, Jesus said to the woman at the well what He says to all of us today: "All who drink of this water will be thirsty again. But whoever takes a drink of the water that I will give him shall never, no never, be thirsty any more. But the water I give him shall become a spring of water welling up (flowing, bubbling), continually within him unto (into, for) eternal life." She answered in a manner the present generation will have to learn how to answer: "Sir, give me this water."

It is when we continually draw from this supernatural source that we can keep on giving our lives away to others without our need for cutting any deals.

That is why my wife could say, "I don't 'need' you, but I 'love' you!" God does not 'need' us; He 'loves' us and 'desires' us, and so develops relationship with us.

> **Humanity consists of two kinds of people: givers and takers.**

His Attributes

God is Eternal—meaning, no beginning or an end. I had a beginning and because of Christ's eternal life in me, I will not have an end. Everlasting life is in me. However, God has no beginning and no ending. He has no birth, and thus, no birthdays. He will never know a funeral. As Psalm 90.2 points out, "He is from everlasting to everlasting."

Everything with God is a now thing. He has been where we've been, is where we are, and is also where we are going to be. He is the Way and He makes a way where there is no way!

Some people make promises and then die before fulfilling them. Not God! I can make plans about the future and fail. But God's plans about the future take the future into consideration because He was already there. I don't know the future, but I know Him who creates a future.

That is why we must take words of prophecy seriously. When God leads an individual to give us what they believe to be a Word from the Lord, we need to listen carefully. God is able to impart His eternal knowledge and wisdom through someone else into our life. God knows of things to come and He often gives us a sense of what they look like. The prophetic word confirms the path that we sense God is leading us on.

I am particularly convinced, on the basis of experience, that God will at least give us a clue into next steps. I may not see the entire picture, but I will get one more dot that can be connected to previous ones that will give me a clearer picture of where I am, where I am going, and what it looks like. God delights in leading us into next steps, and He loves to make those steps firm.

You will remember the game we used to play as kids, where we connected dots and ultimately created a picture. I believe that within time the dots of our life connect and we know who we are, why we are here, and what we are supposed to be doing. The picture, or the way God wants us to serve His purposes, becomes clear.

Life Purpose

It is important that the picture be connected. I have found that enough obedient steps in the right direction have created some clarity for my life. I now know what to say "yes" to and what to say *"no"* to.

I remember an important meeting I had with my church leadership team concerning the building plan for our new facility. We were looking at architectural drawings with two buildings standing side by side, one for administration and one a ministry center, plus a price tag of $1,000,000 (one million) more than we could afford at that time.

The prayer I prayed emerged out of my knowledge of God's eternality. I was led to pray:

> "Father, Ancient of Days, the Alpha and Omega, the One who goes before us and makes a way, so that when we get there, we recognize you have already been there. Time means nothing to you. You have been with us in the past, are present with us now, and are in our future. You are already on our land. You see the building you want built. Would you please tell us what it looks like so that we can build it?"

Within minutes the Lord gave us a word of knowledge: *"build up, not out!"* That word rearranged our thinking and saved us a million dollars. We were able to then proceed with the project under one roof and three stories high.

God is Infinite—meaning, He is without end in Himself. "Because He is infinite, we cannot put measurement upon any of His qualities" (Greg Bitgood, The Attributes of God, page 13). There is absolutely no measure or limitation to His love (Ro 8.35), to His power (Eph 1.19), and His resources (Php 4.19). "But my God shall supply all your need according to His riches in glory by Christ Jesus" (KJV).

> ***I like to think of it as the day we made $1,000,000 in one minute.***

There are things God will ask you to do that will require supernatural supply. God thoroughly delights in making the impossible, possible. One word of infinite wisdom, one touch of His infinite grace, and one encounter with infinite mercy can make all the difference in the world. God wants to do greater things through us, not because we are so great but because the Greater One indwells us (1Jn 4.4).

He wants us to know that though our energies and resources may fail, His do not. Though we may faint and grow weary, and even fall, He will not. Even though we become impatient and even discouraged, He does not. What we can't do for ourselves He does for us, and He does it all with great pleasure. That is the character and nature of the God we serve.

God is Immutable—meaning, God cannot and will not change His character. He is who He is and He will always be who He says (Mal 3.6). He does not have to change: He will never change His nature, His attributes, or His character; though at times God has changed His dealings with men based upon their

Life Purpose

change of heart. Hebrews 13.8 declares: "Jesus Christ, the same yesterday, today, and forever."

God chose a plan, called you to participate in it, knows every eventuality, and He is sticking to it. He is not a man that He should change. We may want to see things changed or we may want God to change our calling, but it is then that our confidence in His immutability must emerge. God will not move from His position so we had better remain steadfast, endure in faith, and wait out the storms because something good, and of God, is going to break out.

Has it occurred to you that nothing ever occurs to Him?

God is Omniscient—meaning, He possesses complete knowledge that is knowable. He does not have to reason because He knows intimately and completely all things (Ps 147.4-5). His thinking vastly supercedes our capabilities: "For My thoughts are not your thoughts, neither are your ways My ways," declares the LORD. "As the heavens are higher than the earth, so are My ways higher than your ways, and My thoughts than your thoughts" (Isa 55.8-9, NIV).

God knows everything that can happen to hinder His plan, and yet, He has decided on a plan and is working the plan. He who "began the good work" is faithful to complete the good work (Php 1.6). The things that are appointed for you will occur: Job 23.14 says, "For He performs what is appointed for me, and many such things are with Him" (NKJV).

God does not set His people up for a disappointment: He sets them up for an appointment with destiny. He knows what lies directly in front of you and has taken into consideration every possible scenario, yet still asks for your participation. His Omniscience brings rest to my soul for He knows things I don't, and I have learned to trust Him.

God is Omnipresent—meaning, God is present at all times, everywhere: in the past, present, and future. Jeremiah 23.23-24 says: "Am I a God at hand . . . and not a God afar off? Can any hide himself in secret places that I shall not see him? saith the LORD. Do not I fill heaven and earth? saith the LORD" (KJV). God lives in heaven, yet resides in our hearts (Eph 1.20; Jn 14.23). Heaven is His throne and the earth is His footstool, but the heart of the humble is still His resting place (Isa 66.1-2).

> **God does not set you up for disappointment, but an appointment with destiny.**

It is really crucial we understand that God does not join us in the midst of our troubles: He was there all along. He didn't join the three Hebrew children in the fiery furnace: He was there before they arrived. They joined Him in the fire and it was His life giving presence that protected them from death. Our own perspective is critical in developing confidence to perform and carry out the will of God.

God is Omnipotent—meaning, God possesses within Himself absolute power and potential to do anything that is within His plan and purpose. Nothing is beyond His ability to act. Psalm 115.3 declares,

Life Purpose

"Our God is in heaven; He does whatever pleases Him" (NIV). He never gets tired or weary (Isa 40.28). His power is ruled by His holiness and in complete compliance with His will. His purpose will come to pass.
Knowing God's divine attributes is essential in pursuing and completing your life assignment.

God's *eternality* means He will never die before the purpose and plan is completed.
God's *infinitude* means He will never tire of you or become impatient with you.
God's *immutability* means He will never change what He has planned for you.
God's *omniscience* means He has thought of every detail and there are no surprises.
God's *omnipresence* means He will be with you always: if you go through the fire, He will be there.
God's *omnipotence* means there is nothing you now face or will face that He has not already faced and conquered for you.

Knowing this will help you confidently pursue His plan for your life and His purpose for your generation. Getting this into your heart will firmly establish you when you face any kind of opposition or obstacle, whether it be from human or demonic origins. You don't run or bolt at the time of the stare down; you move forward into your destiny.
It is not knowing God's will for your life that is important: it is all about knowing God's will, period. It is whether your will is for God. Know God and

you will know His will. It is not simply a matter of locating God's will for you first; it is simply a matter of locating your will for God!

His Character

There are so many characteristics to God, manifested in Christ, His Son. Both the written and the living Word declare who He is. We know Him, yet, we are coming to know Him. This is an eternal process. We simply get glimpses into who He is.

Yet, knowing His character is critical to the success of your life purpose. A lack of understanding the character of God will actually affect the development of your own character and result in actions devoid of spirituality, or morality. God wants His character so deeply imbedded in you so that you can fulfill your life purpose with integrity and dignity.

What are some of those elements of divine character that would be beneficial for you to know and demonstrate through your life on a daily basis?

God is Holy (Isa 57.15)—He will never, never

> **You don't run or bolt at the time of the stare down; you move forward into your destiny.**

ask you to transgress His moral code, either in the expression of who you are or in what you do. His holiness is the key trait of His character, running like a thread through the tapestry of your moral life.

Life Purpose

God is Love (1Jn 4.7-8)—He will never, never ask you to do something that is not rooted in His thinking that this is the most loving thing to do. It is not sentimentality or sloppy agape: it is fully active and directed towards you at all times because that is who He is. Knowing His love will help you to function in His love (Eph 3.16-20).

God is Faithful (Dt 32.4)—"He is the Rock, His works are perfect, and all His ways are just. A faithful God who does no wrong, upright and just is He" (NIV). God will never ask you to do something that He is not faithful in keeping His promise and fulfilling His commitment to perform. Psalm 33.4 states: "He is faithful in all He does" (NIV). He will never let you be tested above what you are able to bear (1Co 10.13).

Why don't you take a few moments and add some of your own personal meaning to these characteristics of God: mercy, peace, joy, friendship, grace, forgiveness.

The more you understand God's character, it seems the more confident you become in listening and submitting to the call of God. The fact that God forgives means there is a second chance in God. The fact that God is an intercessor means that He is praying for you right now. He believes in you and wants to see you succeed and ultimately prevail. The fact that He is patient means He gives you time to emerge and mature.

John speaks of the fathers and says their maturity is really known by one primary characteristic in their life: "[they] have come to know Him who has existed from the beginning" (1Jn 2.14, AMP). Your maturity

86

in God is indispensably connected to your confidence in who you know God to be and how rightly connected that understanding is to truth.

His Ways and Works

The Apostle Paul faithfully prayed the following scripture over the Colossian church: "Be assured that from the first day we heard of you, we haven't stopped praying for you, asking God to give you wise minds and spirits attuned to His will, and so acquire a thorough understanding of how God works.

We pray that you'll live well for the Master, making him proud of you as you work hard in His orchard. As you learn more and more how God works, you will learn how to do *your* work" (Col 1.8-10, TMT).

The more acquainted you become with God's nature, attributes and His character, the more familiar you become with His ways and acts. In a sense, it is like watching humans interact with each other: the closer one person becomes to another, the more predictable their ways and actions are.

Even though God's thoughts and ways are higher than your own, God wants you to come to a place where they, too, are known. Because you know Him, you can discern what God would do and why He would do it. That process will take time and commitment to fully develop: it will require intimacy.

God revealed His works to Israel, but His ways to Moses (Ps 103.7). If He would do this for Moses, a man with whom He spoke face to face (Ex 33.11), He will do the same for you. God wants you tracking

Life Purpose

with Him, and you can, if you will seek His face and not His hand.

> **Don't assume that you know it all.**

Jesus did what He saw the Father doing. God wants to anoint your eyes so that you are able to do what He is doing, just as Jesus did. In John 5.19, Jesus gave them this answer: "I tell you the truth, the Son can do nothing by Himself; He can do only what He sees His Father doing, because whatever the Father does the Son also does" (NIV). Jesus is the example we must follow in our spiritual walk.

The key to successfully fulfilling your life assignment is in learning the kinds of things God would do and the ways He would do them, instead of following your own heart, mind, and fleshly desires. "Trust God from the bottom of your heart; don't try to figure out everything on your own. Listen for God's voice in everything you do, everywhere you go; He's the one who will keep you on track. Don't assume that you know it all" (Pr 3.4-5, TMT).

His Name

Knowing the names of God will help to build your confidence in carrying out His will, in His way.

Knowing He is your *Saviour* should build into you immense confidence that He is there to save you in every circumstance and difficulty that you encounter;

Knowing He is your *Redeemer* should sustain you in every situation when you feel that all is lost and there is no hope or help in the natural realm;

Knowing He is your *Lord* should give you strength to carry on because He is in charge and has the authority to deal with every problem, whether it be of human or demonic design;

Knowing He is your *Shepherd* should give you rest, because He is always leading you and guiding your steps even through the valley of the shadow of death.

Really get to know the names of God. Study them with great care because the Bible is a progressive revelation of God's name. From Adam—to the Church—to us, God is constantly revealing himself. His name has meaning and substance and can be relied upon in days of confusion or trouble.

Call on His name. God says in Jeremiah 33.3: "Call Me, and I will answer thee, and shew thee great and mighty things, which thou knowest not" (KJV). God is able to heal you, for He is your healer. He is willing to deliver you, because He is your deliverer. Call upon the Name of the Lord and receive the answers to your cries for help.

His Voice and Will

When you have matured in the knowledge of God, knowing His voice and doing His will becomes easier and easier. Why? Because you know Him. You have been spending time talking to Him. You know what He wants in the situations that you encounter. You know His heart towards people. You are able to distinguish between His voice and the voice of another.

The Message Translation of Colossians 1.6 says,

Life Purpose

"The lines of purpose in your life never grow slack." Why? Because you know Him and your pursuit of Him has opened up to you an upward call, a future, and a destiny. You have been chosen to participate with Him in an incredible discovery of life and a passionate pursuit of purpose. You are a co-laborer with Him, a companion in the Great Cause, connected by His Spirit and kept by His Word. You have the ear of an eager disciple and delight in doing His will.

> ***The fact that God forgives means there is a second chance in God.***

I exhort you as the Apostle Paul did when he wrote to the Philippians (3.17-19, TMT):

> "I'm not saying that I have this all together, that I have it made. But I am well on my way, reaching out for Christ, who has so wondrously reached out for me. Friends, don't get me wrong: by no means do I count myself an expert in all of this, but I've got my eye on the goal, where God is beckoning us onward—to Jesus. I'm off and running, and I'm not turning back. So let's keep focused on that goal, those of us who want everything God has for us."

God speaks to His people. So train yourself with the ear of a disciple to hear what the Spirit of God is saying. I believe it is not as much an issue of God not talking, as it is a matter of the Church not listening. God wants to reveal to you the mystery of His will.

He wants to give you an understanding of your place under the sun and in the Son. He desires to share with you exactly what He is getting ready to do.

Most of our praying to God amounts to dialing Heaven 911, announcing our needs, requesting His help, and then hanging up. They are nothing more than what my son calls *"prayer flares!"* If we are going to start encountering God, we have to mature beyond prayers of supplication and petition. We need to grow into *"listening prayers."*

Prayer is nothing more than communication with God. When God places me in the presence of someone who has something important to say that I need to hear, I listen up. When I am in the presence of people, such as the Prime Minister or President, then I act appropriately by calling him Mr. Prime Minister or Mr. President. It's a matter of honour and respect. When the creature is talking to the Creator, we need to listen more than talk. When the son is talking to the Dad, he needs to be teachable and not talk so much.

I truly believe that prayer is ten percent talking to God and ninety percent listening. Most of us need to hone our listening skills, spiritually. This is the only way we can fulfill scripture and "pray without ceasing" (1Th 5.17). I can listen all day and be ever ready to respond to Him in the midnight hours.

> *"We have met with God, and He is going to journey with us."*
> Ed Berk

Life Purpose

Chapter 9

What Are You Doing, Lord?

"I felt I was walking with destiny, and that all my past life had been a preparation for this hour and for this trial."

Winston Churchill

What Are You Doing, Lord?
"[Earnestly] remember the former things which I did of old; for I am God, and there is no one else; I am God, and there is none like Me, declaring the end and the result from the beginning and from ancient times the things that are not yet done, saying, 'My counsel shall stand, and I will do all My pleasure and purpose.' Yes, I have spoken, and I will bring it to pass; I have purposed it, and I will do it."

Isaiah 46.9-11, *Amplified Bible*

Early in my walk with God, I was introduced to a very popular Christian tract called *"The Four Spiritual Laws."* While many concepts within it are true and are a valid witnessing tool, I can still remember an experience that challenged my use of it.

I was going through the tract with a young man one day and we came to the part that says, *"God has a wonderful plan for your life."* He suddenly halted our conversation and asked me the question I dreaded he would ask: *"What's God's plan for your life?"* I would like to tell you I had a ready answer, besides the common rebuttal, *"Well, I know I am going to heaven,"* but I didn't. His question and the lack of an answer caused me to never want to be in that position again. I had to know what that "wonderful plan was" and live it out.

I am constantly reminded there are "many plans in a man's mind, but it is the Lord's purpose that will stand" (Pr 19.21). God is a God of purpose. Everything He has in mind from the beginning of time has been planned with intention and reason, to perfection. The Message Translation of Psalm 33.11 states, "God's plan for the world stands up, all His designs are made to last."

> **He suddenly halted our conversation and asked me the question I dreaded he would ask, "What's God's plan for your life?"**

In the last chapter you came to the realization that the more you know God, the more you will trust Him and allow His grace to flow through your life. This enables you to know that He is your forgiveness, always forgiving when you seek it and helping you to face your failures and get up again; He is your redeemer and helps you to face loss and believe

Life Purpose

for restoration; He is your peace and strengthens you in the midst of great confusion; and He is your intercessor, praying to the Father on your behalf. God wants information to turn into a revelation that will affect your life forever. Knowledge can be learned and quickly forgotten, but never a revelation of truth: it becomes wisdom. This wisdom is integrated into your life and transformation occurs. God wants your life conformed to Him so that your world can be revolutionized.

> "It's All About You, Jesus
> My task is to bring out in the open and
> make plain what God, who created
> all this in the first place, has been doing in
> secret and behind the scenes all along.
> Through Christians like yourselves gathered
> in churches, this extraordinary plan
> of God is becoming known and talked
> about even among the angels!
> All this is proceeding along lines planned
> all along by God and then executed in
> Christ Jesus. When we trust in Him, we're
> free to say whatever needs to be said,
> bold to go wherever we need to go."

Ephesians 3.12-15a, *The Message Translation*

I have read much about getting to know God's will for my life. Although much of it has been helpful, it has been my observation that most of it has been written from an incorrect perspective. The focus has been on us and not Him! This Christian life is not about locating God's will for my life; it's all about my will for God's life. It's not the will of God for my life that's important; it's the will of God, period! History making is not about us; it has been, is, and will ever be about Him!

What Are You Doing, Lord?

You see the sobriety of this focus when Christ challenges those people who are desirous of following Him. Matthew 7.21 declares: "Not every one that saith unto me, 'Lord, Lord,' shall enter into the kingdom of heaven; but he that doeth the will of My Father which is in heaven'" (KJV). This is the fundamental truth of the gospel that must be grasped in your heart.

The essence of the Lordship message is that *you were not saved to do your own thing.* You were saved from doing your own thing to doing His thing. You who now know Christ are no longer living for yourselves (2Co 5.15). You no longer have ownership of your life: you now belong to Someone else and have totally surrendered your right to express your own feelings, moods, philosophies, thoughts, ambitions, wants, dreams, ideas, opinions, or desires. Your life is now "hid with Christ in God" (Col 3.3). The life you now live, you live by the faith of the Son of God (Gal 2.20).

> *Knowledge can be learned and forgotten, but never a revelation of truth.*

Life Purpose

Read through the following keys in John 5.17-20 that are connected to Christ pursuing the Father's purpose for His life.

> "My Father has worked [even] until now. He has never ceased working, He is still working—and I too must be at [divine] work... The Son is able to do nothing of His own accord; but He is able to do only what He sees the Father doing. For whatever the Father does is what the Son does in the same way [in His turn]. The Father dearly loves the Son and discloses (shows) to Him everything that He Himself does... and even the greater things (AMP)."

Keys To A Purpose Led Life

The following keys are fundamental to assessing the will of God. If you reject them, you could wind up being rejected and miss out on God's purpose for your life. Is it worth it?

- The Father is at work, now—He is always working.
- You must be busy doing the Father's work.
- You can do nothing successfully on your own.
- You can only do what you see the Father doing.
- The Father loves you as He loved His Son.
- The Father will disclose to you what you should do.
- Even you will do the greater things (Jn 14.12).

The Message Translation of Matthew 7.21-35 affirms these foundational keys.

"Knowing the correct password—saying 'Master, Master,' for instance—isn't going to get you anywhere with me. What is required is serious obedience—doing what my Father wills. I can see it now—at the Final Judgment thousands strutting up to me and saying, 'Master, we preached the Message, we bashed the demons, our God-sponsored projects had everyone talking.' And do you know what I am going to say? 'You missed the boat. All you did was use me to make yourselves important. You don't impress me one bit. You're out of here.'"

It's His Purpose, Not Mine

This is the essence of the Apostle Paul's challenge to the Christian church in Romans 8.28: "And we know that all things work together for good to them that love God, to them who are called according to His purpose" (KJV). The context of this is intercession and prayer, one of the most 'rebellious acts' (in a godly way) that can be committed. Prayer is rebellion against the status quo. It does not stop until things have dramatically changed and aligned themselves to His will.

Many people who read this favourite portion of scripture memorize it up to "love God." However, they fail to connect with the rest of the story: "to them

Life Purpose

who are called according to His purpose." Why is this important? Because there are many people who say they love God but things do not work together for good.

Prayer is rebellion against the status quo.

Let's look at Romans 8.28 more closely.

"We know" (Greek oidamen)—not, we guess or assume, but we know, personally and intimately, through inner belief and observation;
"all things" (Greek panta)—not, some things, but all things, everything, always;
"work together" (Greek sunergei)—cooperate, a root for our word synergy;
"for good" (Greek agathon)—for our benefit, not for our demise;
"to them that love God"—this is not referring to a sentimentality or sloppy agape, but real love. We love God because Jesus said, "If ye love me, keep My commandments" (Jn 14.15, KJV). The highest form of love is obedience;
"that are called" (Greek kleetois)—meaning, "appointed," anointed, positioned, and commissioned by God the Father;
"according to His purpose" (Greek prosthesis)— what is "set forth before God."

Corrie ten Boom's testimony about her deliverance from the sexual advances of the prison guards (during

World War II) places this scripture in context. Corrie had been complaining about the lice in her cell and asking the Lord to deliver her from their bites. In prayer, the Lord revealed to her that He sent the lice to protect her: as long as she had lice, the guards did not want to touch her. Now her complaining was instantly transformed to praise because she had received a revelation of His purpose.

You have not been called according to your purpose: "Father, this is what I believe I am to do. Please bless me!" It is not "I've waited to hear from You, Lord, but because You haven't spoken yet, I believe I need to make this decision." Those scenarios have an element of *ignorance*—you really don't know what it actually means to be called by God, and/or *arrogance*—you really don't care or consider it important that God calls you.

Doing your own will and calling it God's will opens the door for a lot of heartache. Moses had to separate himself from those who assumed they were obeying God in going into the land, when God and the ark of His presence would not go up with them into battle (Nu 14.42-45).

The word *purpose* (Greek prosthesis) means *"a setting forth"* (used of the "shewbread"). We read in Ephesians 1.11 that we have obtained "an inheritance, being predestinated according to the purpose of Him who worketh all things after the counsel of His own will" (KJV). The Message Translation of the same text says, "It's in Christ that we find out who we are and what we are living for. Long before we first heard of Christ and got our hopes up, He had His eye on us, had designs on us for glorious living, part of the overall purpose He is working out in everything and everyone."

What Are You Doing, Lord?

God has set forth what He desires to do. If you work with Him, connect to His will for your life and serve His purpose in this generation, there will be a *synthesis*—or *"a harmony"*—of purpose. If you act independently of His purpose and do your own thing, however good it may be, you will be working in an *antithetical* way to God's purpose and plan, or *"in direct opposition or in contradiction to."*

You have been called for a purpose! You are not here by accident. Your destiny does not come by way of your personal decision or choice: it comes by a continuing discovery. You are a traveler, a sojourner. You are in process. You have begun to run the race in Christ and He is the "Author and the Finisher of your faith" (Heb 12.2).

> ***In prayer, the Lord revealed to her that He had sent the lice to protect her.***

The purpose of God, as the shewbread, is found in the holy place. Used twelve times in scripture, it refers to what man is unable to do (Ac 27.12-20) outside of God's grace and power. Like the shewbread, His will must become our bread (Jn 4.34).

If you want things to work together for your good, it is vital that you seriously consider getting to know what God is doing, His plan and purpose, and do it! It is a sobering thought that things may not work together for your good just because you say you are a Christian or 'love' God.

How God's Purpose Works

To grasp the purposeful nature of God, it is important we build a theological foundation of terms that many of us pass over because they seem deep and irrelevant. However, they form the foundation of our belief system. We would not dare to build the superstructure of a home without making sure that the foundation is established and strong. I am convinced that weak theological foundations in believers undermine their progress in kingdom purpose and endurance in faith.

Knowing these biblical terms will bring peace to your heart and mind and cause your understanding of personal purpose to be developed. An ignorance of these terms will leave you open to the inroads of darkness and death, where ideas reign that are contrary to the truth of God (2Co 10.3-5).

You will remember Solomon's dilemma, trying to find a reason for his existence. He comes to believe there exists a time for everything under Heaven. He falls back on a concept that has been coined the *sovereignty of God* in the affairs of men! God orders everything that happens and there is nothing man can

Life Purpose

do to hinder [or help]—the clock is always ticking and no one can interfere with anything He has planned. Many theologians have explored, in depth, man's response to this conclusion. Their interpretations influence how we will perceive life and living, and also where we will draw the line concerning responsibility for the events of life. This has led to a description of life through the lenses of *two* theological extremes.

In the first place, all of life is *completely controlled by God*. No matter what you do, the result has already been established: God is sovereign. It is "que sera, sera—whatever will be, will be. The future's not ours to see—que sera, sera." This view often leads to apathetic indifference, at best, and Christian fatalism, at worst.

In the second place, all of life is based upon *free, moral choice*. Man has the capacity to reject God's plan and purpose for his life: essentially, man is sovereign. This perspective can breed rebellion, selfishness, and a resistance to the purpose of God; resenting His sovereignty or His right to interfere.

This dilemma can be seen in the Apostle Paul's address to King Agrippa when he contends that he was "not disobedient to the heavenly vision" (Ac 26.19), meaning, he could have been! As you process this theologically, you may come to the conclusion that the will of God is not as hard to find as it is so difficult to obey! Your problem may not be ignorance as much as disobedience, for it would be difficult for God to hold you accountable and guilty of disobedience to His will when it was not revealed to you. That kind of judgment would be against God's character.

> **Like the images of a coin, truth has two faces.**

As I share with you the following Biblical truths, some of your foundational beliefs are going to be challenged. And that is my intent. An introduction to these theological building blocks is by no means exhaustive, but they are given as simply as I can possibly introduce them. Understand that all truth is in divine tension. Like the images of a coin, there is truth with two faces.

For years now theologians have been arguing over this issue. One would see the face side of a coin and argue that it is a face. The other would see the animal side of a coin and argue that it is an animal. Both positions are true together, without compromise. They are not in opposition or contradiction. They simply are both true together and provide a complete picture. We need to look at the whole and stop arguing.

I am convinced that God's sovereignty has to do with His eternal purpose and plan. Man can choose to reject the will of God, but that will not change it or interfere with His intentions or implementation. God loves us and has a part for us to play in bringing to pass His will. If we decline, God will raise up someone else.

Life Purpose

A Life Purpose Study of King Saul

Every once in a while we read about an individual's life where we are tempted to question the goodness or the integrity of God. It appears, at first glance, that particular individual has been set up by God to fail. Saul is one of those people I was perplexed about. Let's look at Saul's background to try and help us understand the dilemma of the above question.

When Israel was developing as a nation, their moral, social, and spiritual life was being overseen by judges who were appointed by God. In Saul's day Samuel was recognized as the nation's authority under God. However, Samuel's sons did not carry a similar anointing and the people began to desire "a king to rule over [them] like all the other nations" (1Sa 8.5). Samuel viewed this as an attempt to undermine the authority of God, who was their King (verse 7).

However, though it was not the "perfect will of God" for the nation of Israel, God permitted their pursuit of a king—it was "the acceptable will of God" (Ro 12.1-2). Read through 1 Samuel 8. Permission was granted, but it included a warning as to what a king may do. Nevertheless, they wanted a king "to govern us and go out before us and fight our battles." So it was within this context that Samuel is commissioned by God to seek out a king for the people of Israel.

1 Samuel 9 reveals a little of Saul's background: he was the son of Kish, a Benjamite, a mighty man

of wealth and valour. He was choice and more handsome than all the men of Israel, a head taller than any of the people. He was not afraid of work: for example, he was commissioned one day to find his father's donkeys. He had a humble appreciation of his place within Israel (his family was the least of the clan's families).

In locating the family's donkeys he is led to Samuel, a seer and a man of God. God prepares Samuel's heart for Saul's arrival. God appoints Samuel to anoint Saul as leader over God's people, to walk in God's authority, and to save them from the hand of their enemies—the Philistines.

Saul leaves home one fine day to fulfill a mundane act of servanthood and returns home anointed to be king. Read 1 Samuel 10 for the complete account. Samuel anoints Saul to be king by the Word of the Lord. He also tells Saul about the spiritual experiences he is about ready to have. When Saul left Samuel's presence, *"God gave him another heart."* When Saul met up with the prophetic band, "the Spirit of the Lord came upon him mightily . . . he was turned into another man . . . and he spoke under divine inspiration."

> **Saul is found hiding in the baggage. This speaks of inadequacy, like many God has called.**

When Saul was asked where he had been, we see the integrity of the man: "But of the matter of

Life Purpose

the kingdom, of which Samuel spoke, he told him nothing." He does not toot his own horn. When Samuel assembles the people together to introduce them to their newly crowned king, Saul is found hiding in the baggage. This speaks of inadequacy, like so many that God has called. When Saul is presented to the people, he is surrounded by "a band of valiant men whose hearts God had touched." When despised by other men and given no gift from them as king, he held his peace and did not abuse his authority.

Saul's Three Tests

His *first* test was with Nahash the Ammonite. Read 1 Samuel 11 and 12. "The spirit of the Lord came mightily upon him when he heard the tidings, and his anger was greatly kindled." God led him forth in great triumph. When Saul's victory was complete, he had the opportunity to seek revenge upon those who had despised his calling, but again, his character came through.

God establishes a covenant with Saul and with the people. The rule is absolutely clear: "If you will revere and fear the Lord and serve Him and hearken to His voice and not rebel against His commandment, and if both you and your king will follow the Lord your God, it will be well." Samuel affirms God's mercy towards them and in His covenant to bless and instruct them in the good and right way.

His *second* test came against the Philistines. Read 1 Samuel 13. Men who had gathered with him ran away and hid or they deserted: the remaining few were fearful and scattering. Saul thought he could enter into a dimension of ministry that was ordered for Samuel, that of the priesthood and offering up the sacrifice out of concern over morale and fear of diminishment: for example, 30,000 men to 600. The judgment was swift and severe: "You have not kept the Lord's commandment . . . for the Lord would have established your kingdom over Israel forever; but now your kingdom will not continue." He is to be replaced. His kingdom will not continue.

Acts 13.22 declares emphatically that God deposed Saul: "And when He had deposed Saul, He raised up David to be their king; of him He bore witness and said, 'I have found David the son of Jesse a man after My own heart, who will do all My will and carry out My program fully.'"

From that point forward, Saul fought courageously against the enemies of Israel. However, whenever he saw "any mighty or [outstandingly] courageous man, he quickly attached him to himself" (1Sa 14.52). This speaks of insecurity.

Saul's third test came against Agag, the king of the Amalekites. Read 1 Samuel 15. Again, Saul fails the test by not completely fulfilling God's command. He spares the best of what has been captured. When he is in trouble with the prophet Samuel for his lack of obedience, he passes the buck. He has lost a sense of humility and traded it for the security of numbers following him as king. Consequently, Saul is denied his kingship over Israel and the kingdom is stripped

Life Purpose

from him. "The Spirit of the Lord departed from Saul, and an evil spirit from the Lord tormented and troubled him" (1Sa 16.14).

> ***I have found David the son of Jesse a man after my own heart.***

Instead of waging war against the Philistines as the Lord had purposed him to do, we find Saul waiting for a leader to emerge to fight his fight. He has lost his sense of anointing, the presence of God, and his ability to lead. He is now hanging on, rather than yielding his call and appointment to God who gave him his position.

David is raised up by God to replace Saul. Jonathan, Saul's son, recognizes the transfer of anointing upon David's life (1Sa 18.1-5). Saul attempts to kill David. However, we see God's merciful hand again visiting Saul at Naioth in Ramah when His Spirit comes upon him and he prophesies (1Sa 19.23-24). Saul knows about this transference of power (1Sa 24.17-20). His life ends in disgrace entertaining a medium (1Sa 28) and by committing suicide on the battlefield (1Sa 31.4). It was a tragic end to a great start.

God has established a purpose that involves all people and nations. Saul intersected God's purpose for a nation and found his own purpose in life—he departed as a servant and came back a king.

God calls us to be a part of His purpose in spite of our own personal problems and inadequacies. He doesn't leave us to fend for ourselves, but He equips us with everything that we need to succeed and be prosperous.

God is fair. The playing field is level for every participant. Playing by the rules (God's agenda and obedience); bearing personal responsibility (no blame shifting); and allowing a replacement (standing behind others and joyfully seeing them succeed) are key components to finishing the game. However, on the downside to this is disqualification (because of sin and disobedience) to complete the game which can affect many generations to come.

Saul is a picture of one who began his life with incredible promise and clarity of purpose. It appears that he may have blundered into His life assignment; however, God was totally committed to using him for the long haul to establish the nation state of Israel in the midst of their enemies. God was willing to continue leading them into victory after victory. It was Saul's lack of pursuit or obedience to the call and purpose of God that affected his life, his son Jonathan's life, and also his family for generations to come. This is a very sobering but also non-prejudicial ending to a man's life. He could probably have been one of the Bible's greatest success stories.

With that in mind, let's take a look at some fundamental life purpose building blocks.

Theological Building Blocks

Firstly, *foreordination*: [foreordained] meaning, "to determine or fix beforehand!" God possesses the

Life Purpose

capability to provide whatever is necessary for the continuation of the universe that He created: this He does with infinite precision. God planned: the universe was no accident; nothing was left to fate or chance. God predetermined a purpose and a plan, and then He chose just those things that would promote only what He had predetermined!

God has the ability to create a plan for all people, at all times, in all generations, in all nations, and bring that plan to fruition. Our foreordination powers are limited by our lack of divinity. God is God, and He is able to "plan His work and then work His plan!"

> ***The playing field is level for every participant.***

God was not caught by surprise at any rebellion against His purpose (for example, Lucifer and Adam) because He has "worked all things according to the good pleasure of His will" (Eph 1.5). In 1 Corinthians 2.7-8, the Apostle Paul alluded to the foreordination of God: "But we speak the wisdom of God in a mystery, even the hidden wisdom, which God ordained before the world unto our glory: which none of the princes of this world knew: for had they known it, they would not have crucified the Lord of glory" (KJV).

Galatians 4.4 says that Jesus came in the *"fullness of time."* Jesus came right on time: He was in the right place at the right time, with the right people, saying and doing the right things. He was crucified at the right time (Ac 2.23; 4.27-28). However, even though

Jesus was privy to part of the Father's purpose for His life, His natural man did not know more than His Father revealed to Him. "But of that day and hour knoweth no man, no, not the angels of heaven, but My Father only" (Mt 24.36, KJV).

Secondly, *decree*: meaning, "the very act by which God has established the certainty of what He has predetermined, planned!" It was by foreordination that God established His purpose; by decree, He establishes the certainty of that same purpose. God settled upon one plan. He then established it by an irreversible decree. "Thou shalt also decree a thing, and it shall be established unto thee" (Job 22.28, KJV).

Daniel 11.36 declares:

> "And the king shall do according to his will; and he shall exalt himself, and magnify himself above every god, and shall speak marvellous things against the God of gods, and shall prosper till the indignation be accomplished: for that which is determined shall be done" (KJV).

Whatever a natural king decreed, it became law in the land and every authority worked together to put the law into effect. When the King of Kings speaks in the heavens, a matter is done: "Forever, O Lord, thy word is settled in heaven" (Ps 119.89, KJV).

Note: the permissive decrees of God—though God foresaw sin's entrance into the universe, He merely permitted it: He did not decree or cause it! He can, therefore, foresee how men will act or react to the message of His grace without decreeing how they will act and plan accordingly. God's selection of men is based upon His foreknowledge.

Thirdly, *foreknowledge:* meaning, "what God knows will come to pass because of His decree!" God calls people to serve His purpose within their generation, but appreciating man's free and moral choice—it's His purpose that is foreknown and most important.

Foreknowledge is simply "the unique knowledge of God which enables Him to know all events, including the free acts of man, before they happen" (*Nelson's Illustrated Bible Dictionary,* Copyright ©1986, Thomas Nelson Publishers). Please note: God's foreknowledge is more than foresight. God does not know future events and the actions of men because He foresees them; He knows them because He wills them to happen (Ps 139.15-16).

Let me use a personal illustration that clarifies this concept of foreknowledge in a limited way. When our three children were younger, my wife did a lot of baking. She would put the cookies on the counter and leave the kitchen. We both knew what was going to happen. Sure enough, when we left, they invaded the kitchen and took some cookies. We didn't make them take the cookies, but we knew them well enough to assess what they would do. God knows what we will do; however, He does not interfere with our choices. We are free to choose.

> **We didn't make them take the cookies, but we knew them well enough to assess what they would do.**

God's foreknowledge is an act of His will. Isaiah 41.4 says, "Who has performed and done it, calling the generations from the beginning? 'I, the LORD, am the first; and with the last I am He'" (NKJV).

There is no question that you have the capability and the capacity of disappointing and grieving Him. You can opt out of the process: you can remove yourself from participating in the fulfillment of His purpose in your time. You can interfere with your own personal destiny by rejecting God's purpose! You have the ability to thwart the grace of God!

God has an eternal plan and purpose that He is bringing to fulfillment. He is the history maker. Man cannot interfere with that process. However, God has chosen to bring it about through people. Can He count on you hearing and obeying His call? His purpose will be accomplished—will you be there at the finish line?

> **Get to know God. Grow with God.**
> **God knows what He is doing**
> **And where He is going!**

Life Purpose

Chapter 10

You Called, God?

"What is life's heaviest burden? Having nothing to carry."

"To be honest, one of my motives in making so much money was simple—to have the money to hire people to do what I don't like doing. But there's one thing I've never been able to hire anyone to do for me: find my own sense of purpose and fulfillment. I'd give anything to discover that!"

(Quote from a prominent businessman)
Os Guiness, *The Call* (page 1)

In Os Guiness' book *The Call,* he quotes Frydor Dostoevsky's The Brothers Karamazov and their terrifying account of what will happen to the human soul when it doubts its purpose: "For the secret of man's being is not only to live—but to live for something definite. Without a firm notion of what he is living for, man will not accept life and will rather destroy himself than remain on earth."

The call of God means that "a universal summons to receive His grace and to yield ourselves to being part of His great purpose has gone out to every man, woman, and child." The call is to all, to every individual to receive His grace (Tit 2.11). Paul declared in 1 Timothy 2.4, 6: "God wishes all men to be saved and know the Truth . . . [and so] gave Himself to be a ransom for all people."

God is no respecter of persons.

Peter gently reminds us in 2 Peter 3.9:

> "God does not delay and is not tardy or slow about what He promises, according to some people's conception of slowness, but He is longsuffering (extraordinarily patient) toward you, not desiring that any should perish, but that all should turn to repentance (AMP)."

Hebrews 2.9 affirms that He experienced death for every individual. His death, John says, was not just for our sins "but also the sins of the whole world" (1Jn 2.2).

God is no respecter of persons, willing that some are saved and others lost, while some have a life purpose and others live without this crucial ingredient. This concept of God is against everything we have learned about His nature and character. The parable on grace Jesus gives in Matthew 20 speaks of His right to hire anyone, anytime, for any amount He deems and all receiving the same wage. This doesn't make sense in the vocational world, but it does to God's world and His Kingdom.

Life Purpose

I have read a multitude of definitions about God's call upon our life, but Os Guiness defines the call like none other I have ever read. He writes:

"Calling is the truth that God calls us to Himself so decisively that everything we are, everything we do, and everything we have is invested with a special devotion and dynamism lived out as a response to His summons and service" (*The Call*, page 4).

Isn't that quite the statement?

There is no calling without a caller! Absolutely none. We are addressed as individuals, treated with respect and dignity, valued for our uniqueness, and free to respond to the call. The call is for a reason and a season. The fact this call goes out to many people and they live their life with a profound sense of meaning, by responding to it, is a matter of historical record.

"God Almighty has set before me two great objects, the suppression of the Slave Trade and the Reformation of Manners—in modern terms, 'habits, attitudes, morals.'"
William Wilberforce, *Journal*

"God gives a work of passion to those He trusts. I just wish He wouldn't trust me so much."
Mother Teresa

I am convinced you will serve somebody's purpose for your life. Who is that someone going to be? What call are you going to respond to? Because "there is always one moment in childhood when the door opens and lets the future in" (Graham Greene, *The Power and the Glory*).

The Message Translation of Romans 6.21-23 says:

> "You know well enough from your own experience that there are some acts of so-called freedom that destroy freedom. Offer yourselves to sin, for instance, and it's your last free act. But offer yourselves to the ways of God and the freedom never quits. All your lives you've let sin tell you what to do. But thank God that you've started listening to a new Master, One whose commands set you free to live openly in His freedom."

There are some aspects to the call that are shared by all of us in common. There are other aspects that are attached to a very specific plan and unique life assignment for every individual.

> ***Everybody will serve somebody. Who will that somebody be?***

The Common Call

Scripture makes it clear that we all share, in a general sense, the call of God. We have already said

Life Purpose

that deep in every heart is this innate call to locate something worth living, and possibly, dying for. Can you say that about your life?

The call is common to all because God has called each of us (Ro 1.5-6) into companionship and participation with His Son, Jesus (1Co 1.9).

We are all called by His grace and mercy (2Ti 1.9) into one body (1Co 12.13-27) and into liberty (Gal 5.13). We have been called out of darkness into His marvelous light (1Pe 2.9) and into His glorious kingdom (1Th 2.12).

We are called regardless of our status or station in life (1Co 1.26-29) to follow in His footsteps (1Pe 2.21) and lay hold of eternal life (1Ti 6.12).

Called From the Womb

I believe that the call of God is on our life from the womb (Ps 139.13-17). That belief transcends whether you are saved or not saved. Every person alive has been called and gifted by God. When we meet our Creator, the call and gifting that is without repentance is placed into His service from out of the world.

There are many biblical illustrations that affirm this truth and because God is no respecter of persons, I, too, believe each one of us is similarly positioned. Samson—child to Manoah and his wife, wholly devoted before conception to the Lord and His purpose (Jdg 13).

- Samuel—spiritual parents Elkanah and

Hannah regarding the sense of a divine mission for Samuel's life before his conception (1Sa 1–2).
- Jeremiah—"Before I formed you in the womb I knew and approved of you [as My chosen instrument], and before you were born I separated and set you apart, consecrating you and I appointed you a prophet to the nations" (Jer 1.5).
- Isaiah—"the Lord has called me from the womb, from the body of my mother He has named my name" (Isa 49.1, 5).
- John the Baptist—son of Zachariah and Elizabeth, the forerunner of the Lord, prophesied over on the eighth day during circumcision (Lk 1.57-80).
- Paul—"But when He Who had chosen and set me apart [even] before I was born and called me" (Gal 1.15).

This last illustration is unique because we all know about Paul's conversion account as an adult (Ac 9). However, Paul makes it clear that he believed his conversion experience was the moment he understood the call of God upon his life.

Note: It appears that even though there had been a prophetic confirmation about conception, birth, and life assignment, not everyone was made aware of it until there was a specific level of spiritual maturity or conversion experience. I believe all of us have a call from the womb. Just as a natural father has plans for

Life Purpose

his child, so the Heavenly Father has had plans for each of His children from before the foundations of the world were laid.

The Nature of the Call

God saved us and called us not according to works, but to His purpose and grace (2Ti 1.9). He calls us to be found faithful in our call (Rev 17.14); to walk worthy (Eph 4.1); to abide in the calling (1Co 7.20), straining forward to obtain the goal to win the prize (Php 3.12-14). And that calling is irrevocable (Ro 11.29).

Israel (Eze 16; Ro 11) rejected its initial calling and gifting. Consequently, it was lost to the present work of Jesus Christ. However, because of God's grace and His irrevocable call and gifting, she will be grafted in again. You, too, can share in that same grace. If you have been called and not heeded (Pr 1.24), come back and begin to function again. There is no time like the present. Return to Him and give yourself a fresh start.

Do What You Are

Each of us has a tremendous inner compulsion to see our lives count for something. Not one of us has escaped the tendency to compare ourselves to others, to compete with our fellow human beings, and, perhaps, to fight for power and control. This is called *"success motivation"* in the business world; and, in humanity, "the pursuit of happiness."

Sometimes we achieve and succeed: sometimes we fall short of our goals and fail. Other times we exchange our many successes for another kind of bondage; tenaciously hanging on to our achievements or worshiping the past. And, at times, we may even give up and stay down for the count.

The *quest for significance* crosses every boundary line: it touches man and woman; the educated or uneducated; wealthy or poor—it is a human drive because of human need! The principle of upward mobility impacts us everywhere we look: almost everyone, everywhere, is affected by this drive to "get ahead," to fulfill something larger than we are, and to play a part that will make a difference.

We all would like to believe that life, especially our life, has been suited to a personal mission.

Work as a Call or Mission

When the word mission is used and attached to the concept of work, it has been specifically identified as a religious concept. Webster's Dictionary has defined it as "a continuing task or responsibility that one is destined or fitted to do or has been specifically called upon to undertake."

Historically, mission carries with it two specific synonyms: *calling and destiny. Calling* presupposes that (S)omeone calls. Destiny implies (S)omeone is involved and determining our destination for us.

Writers who are genuinely concerned about our society are constantly talking about these

Life Purpose

concepts and often allude to the spirituality of work. Remember the Faith Popcorn quote? "Reaching back to their spiritual roots, [people] look for what was comforting, valuable, and spiritually grounded in the past in order to be secure in the future" (*Clicking*, page 105). People are trying to find and put the soul back into work. That requires a ruthless investigation into who we are.

> **We would like to believe that our life has been suited to a personal mission.**

Who Are You?

Socrates stated, *"An unexamined life is not worth living!"* I believe each one of us was created with a definite purpose in mind. All of nature reveals knowing purpose and assignment in life. The sun knows what to do to stay within its orbit. The seed knows what it is going to be when it grows up. Salmon know how to return to the streams and creeks where they were born. I cannot believe we were created without that inner drive to know and then, to do, our own life purpose.

I believe that we were all created for a special purpose, a purpose that can be known. For some, education is the process of discovery used to find life's purpose. For others, it is work, or friendship, or religion. I am fully persuaded that our sense of mission and destiny is found in a relationship with only one person: God.

We have been given great potential for learning and acquiring knowledge. However, unlike other species, we have not been born with the knowledge and skills to survive; take for example, the animal kingdom. They must be acquired. When that knowledge is acquired we are able to develop skills and abilities that can solve human problems, such as dentists solving teeth problems and mechanics solving car problems.

We become known for the kinds of problems we solve. That has led some to conclude, we are what we do! There is some truth to that. However, I am inclined to believe we must first locate who we are before we do what we do. I am wholly confident we should do what we are, but that will take quite the process of ruthless discovery. We should not determine our work and then be known for who we are by what we do; we should first discover who we are called to be, then release the gifts within us so what we do is an extension of who we are.

Identity, Purpose, and Destiny

For clarification, identity is who we are and it is important that we find our identity in a personal relationship to God, our Creator, who knows each of us intimately.

Purpose is what we have been assigned to do on a daily, seasonal, or lifetime level. Purpose can be found only in the assignments that God gives to us as He unveils what He wants us to do and where we fit. Destiny has to do with where we are going and how we know we have arrived. Destiny is in His hands, for He alone knows the path we are to take and how He is going to get us to our destination.

A traveller engaged a guide to take him across a desert area. When the two men arrived at the edge of the desert, the traveller, looking ahead, saw before them trackless sand without a single footprint, path, or marker of any kind. Turning to his guide, he asked in a tone of surprise, "Where is the road?" With a reproving glance, the guide replied, "I am the road." So too is the Lord our way through unfamiliar territory.

Illustrations for Biblical Preaching (page 421)

David Kalamen

Chapter 11

Where Did You Say We're Going?

"Predestination"

In a Peanuts comic strip there was a conversation between Lucy and Charlie Brown. Lucy said that life is like a deck chair. Some place it so they can see where they are going, some place it so they can see where they have been, and some place it where they are at present. Charlie Brown replied, "I can't even get mine unfolded."

Illustrations for Biblical Preaching (page 219)

Predestination:
"to decide beforehand"

Alice in Wonderland said to Cheshire Cat, "Would you tell me please which way I ought to go from here?" Cheshire Cat said, "That depends where you want to get to." Alice responded, "I don't much care where." Cheshire Cat then replied, "Then it doesn't matter which way you go."

Illustrations for Biblical Preaching (page 254)

Life Purpose

The word predestination from my perspective has often been very misunderstood and misapplied by the Christian community. There are quite a few believers who are under the impression that some people are destined to go to hell as their lot in life, and some will go to heaven. Even those in the world believe that some will be saved and some will be lost. This theological belief system can't be supported by what we know about God's character.

The scriptural use of predestination is always connected to the many benefits that we are entitled and destined to enjoy after we respond to God's call upon our lives and become one of Christ's followers or disciple. This expression is never used as a precondition for our salvation.

Let me illustrate. You are going on a pre-planned holiday to some very remote, tropical vacation resort. You need to get a passport or visa and an airline ticket before you go. When you arrive at the airport, your ticket specifies a time to leave, an airline carrier, and a certain destination. Once approved, you can board the airplane. Once on board, your life has now been predestined. You will be going where the plane is going.

> **Every person has been summoned to go with God to a certain destination.**

This is true regarding your faith. Every person has been summoned to go with God to a certain destination. Those who respond to the call and obey His Word are invited to join Him on this journey.

Once approved, and en route, there are some aspects of your life that are predetermined for you: you are adopted into His family (Eph 1.5); you obtain an inheritance reserved for family (Col 3.23-24); you will be conformed into the character of God (Ro 8.29); and, you will go to the same destination His family is headed toward—heaven (2Pe 3.13).

I believe every life has been created with His purpose. No life is an accident! God has a plan, a good plan, for every single person. He is no respecter of persons. Whatever God does is good, to bring us hope and a future. No individual is exempt from His good intention concerning them. If they surrender to God, and humble themselves, He will raise them up and cause their life to take on divine significance, either in the religious realm or the secular realm of service.

There are some people who question these statements because every once in a while we see an individual's life where we are tempted to question the goodness, or the integrity of God. It appears, at first glance, they have been set up by God to fail. One person who fits that category is Judas. His life story has really challenged my thinking, but it has also helped me to understand God's heart in this matter of predestination. So let's look at the life of Judas, the disciple who betrayed Christ.

Judas

God established an eternal purpose before the foundations of the world. He decreed that purpose

Life Purpose

into being ("His-story"). He knows with certainty what He has declared will occur, and He calls us to participate with him and "serve the purposes of God in this generation!" If we respond to Him—confess our sins, repent, forsake, believe—He predestines us to do those works we were created to do before we were born (Eph 2.10). Our lives will take on divine significance.

If we align our lives to His purpose, we can be assured all things will work out together for good (Ro 8.28). His plan will be lived out through us and our lives will bring Him glory.

Of all the Bible characters, none is more vilified than Judas Iscariot. John calls him "the son of perdition" (Jn 17.12). And Mark comments that "it would have been better for that man if he had not been born" (Mk 14.21). Luke calls him "a traitor" (Lk 6.16). It appears very clear: someone had to betray Christ. Judas seemed destined (Jn 13.18, "chosen"). Like King Saul, it appears the odds have been stacked against him. Kenneth J. Zanca who wrote the book *The Judas Within* makes some extremely interesting observations about Judas' life.

On the surface Judas appears transparently evil. He is viewed as an accomplice to the high priests, the specific possession of the devil, and an instrument of the will of God; elected, so to speak, to fail! Like a character in Greek tragedy, scripture reveals the fate of Judas and then, it appears, we are able to see a pre-ordained destiny emerge.

David Kalamen

> **On the surface Judas appears transparently evil.**

Medieval religious drama pictures Judas as a villain. Da Vinci's Last Supper seats him far away from Christ and most unattractive. He is pictured as sinister, the one who served as guide to those who arrested Jesus (Ac 1.16). Rightly or wrongly, Judas has become an archetype of anyone who betrays and breaks allegiances. Many, throughout history, have attempted to understand this man. Various interpretations have been espoused.

In Robinson Jeffers' play *Dear Judas* (1928)—he pictures Judas frightened by the violence of Jesus (for example, the attack in the Temple, inciting revolt) and betrays Christ by a desire to save innocent blood.

In *The Last Temptation of Christ* (1960), Nikos Kazantzakis pictures a Judas sickened by the gentleness of Jesus Christ, a political extremist, a man yearning for an earthly Messiah, someone who first liberates the state, then the soul. He is quite repulsed by having to love the Roman. He is a nationalist. Judas betrays Christ because He has betrayed the cause.

In the rock opera *Jesus Christ Superstar* (1960s), Judas is pictured as one who does not believe in the deity of Christ. He is concerned only about his own reputation and saving his own life. He betrays to change sides and also maintain public order.

In Anthony Burgess and Franco Zeffirelli's *Jesus of Nazareth,* Judas is portrayed as an intelligent, politically active, but very moderate man who was duped by the Sanhedrin into thinking that the cause would flounder if Christ was not linked to the inner religious circle. He is sold out and throws back the money given to him.

However, we have to remember that Judas' attraction to Jesus was not abnormal. The report concerning Christ had gone throughout the countryside (Lk 4.14). People started associating and identifying with Christ and His Cause (the Kingdom) en masse. The land languished for some spiritual leadership. The people were looking for a political answer to their situation, a military commander, a Saviour.

The Gospels tell us very little about Judas' background except to say he was known as Iscariot and son of Simon (Jn 12.4). The land of Judea was a great distance from Galilee. Judas was politically active. Iscariot, from the Latin word sicarius means *"dagger man!"* It was a Latin name for a member of a nationalist Jewish group related to the Zealots.

There was something about Jesus that put a fire in Judas. There was something in Judas that Jesus loved. They were to become friends who walked with each other for three years.

The Call

It is clear that Jesus called each of His disciples (Jn 6.70). Judas is the last one called and he is the only one to receive an immediate description:

betrayer (Mt 10.4); a traitor (Lu 6.16); a devil (Jn 6.70). It would be beneficial for us to remember these Gospels are written after Christ's death.

Remember, Judas was called to do the same things that the other disciples were called to do (Mt 10.7-8), fully authorized and commissioned to represent the Lord. He was a trusted friend and a personal emissary of Christ. He worked without pay and went without (Mt 10.8-10). Christ thanks the Father for each one of them in His prayer (Jn 17) and He rejoices with them in their achievements (Lu 10.17-19). However, something happened within this man to violate God's purpose in his life.

> **Judas was free to be both disciple and thief.
> Both lived on the inside of him.**

The Gifting

There is only one mention of a specific assignment given to any of the Twelve disciples and that pertains to Judas. In an anointing which prefigures the rites of Christ's burial, a rather questionable woman pours expensive ointment on the Lord's feet and wipes them dry with her hair. The reaction at the scene was unanimous: all were "indignant" (Mt 26.8). John attributes Judas' reaction to another motivation: "he carried the money bag" (Jn 12.6) (that is to say, he was the treasurer). Why Judas was trusted by the group and not Levi, who was the professional

Life Purpose

moneyman, we do not know. It sounded as if he was the more practical and business-minded one of the twelve. Regardless, Judas was free to be both disciple and thief. Both lived on the inside of him.

The Plot

It had appeared to the disciples that as they walked with Christ, He was invincible. Their revelation into His true identity came in Matthew 16: He was "the Christ, the Son of the living God." In the same breath, Jesus outlined His destiny: Jerusalem, suffer many things at the hands of the scribes and Pharisees, and be killed. The shock was visible: Peter's response; and Christ's rebuke. Over and over again Christ outlines this destiny to the chagrin of the disciples. He will be done in by His enemies, but betrayed by a friend.

After the Temple affair, the Temple hierarchy thought of ways to kill Him (Mk 11.18). After raising Lazarus from the dead, they feared Him even more and plotted to take His life (Jn 11.47-53). Even Temple guards were sent to arrest Him but were unsuccessful (Jn 7.32). All the Gospels speak of Christ's enemies scheming against His life (Mt 26.3-5; Mk 14.1-2; Lu 22.1-6; Jn 11.47-53). Their plan was very elementary: arrest Jesus quickly, quietly, and kill Him. The plot was there before it entered into Judas' mind!

The Betrayal

Every Gospel account indicates that the disciples

were shocked by the betrayal coming from within the Twelve. From Luke and John's position, Judas' motivation was Satan entering into him (Lu 22.3; Jn 13.2, 27). From Matthew's perspective, it was greed for money (Mt 26.15).

However, the fee—thirty pieces of silver, the price given by law to the owner of a slave who had died accidently—hardly seems a sufficient cause. He threw the money back! Maybe Judas saw the power turning sides and jumped ship. Maybe he was bribed and his loyalty bought.

And the idea of the Evil One did influence Judas (Lu 4.13), but could he have controlled him? It is questionable!

I believe Judas did not want Christ to die; therefore, he forced a military altercation. The disciples had left the Upper Room armed. Peter pulled his sword and used it to protect Christ. So, some of the other disciples had also been thinking of establishing an Israeli military kingdom other than Judas Iscariot, the nationalist. Judas was deceived by an agenda that ran crosscurrent to Christ's agenda. It is possible that Simon Peter was also targeted; therefore, we understand Christ's rebuke in Matthew 16: "Get behind me, satan!"

> ***Christ was done in by His enemies, but betrayed by His friend.***

Life Purpose

The Covenantal Meal

The Last Supper covenant meal, intended to celebrate the Passover, was a festive time for the disciples. They were in the Holy City; they were together. Jesus ate this meal with all Twelve disciples (Mt 26.20). Though Judas had already agreed to betray Christ, he was there. Jesus is pictured as being in total command of the impending situation. The time of His betrayal is at hand. He announces it and sadness enters the room (Mk 14.19).

One by one, each disciple asks the question: *"Is it I?"* They do not ask, *"Who is it?"* They all personally assess their own hearts. Each one, within time, would abandon Christ in one way or another. The food is placed on the table in a series of dishes (which was the custom of the day) and they eat from the same dish which was a customary sign of fellowship, trust, community, and covenant.

Christ states, "He who dipped his hand in the dish with me shall betray Me" (Mt 26.23). It could have been any one of them. It appears that none of them caught on it was Judas! Jesus gives a morsel of bread to Judas and says, "What you are going to do, do quickly" (Jn 13.27). But no one caught onto what Jesus meant. Maybe He had sent Judas on an errand!

Before Judas left, Jesus broke bread and shared wine with His betrayer. After this was done, they sang together and then went to the Mount of Olives where Jesus prayed often (Jn 18.2; Lu 22.39). In the commotion, Judas slips away into the night.

The death of Christ was inevitable, but His betrayal was not! Judas may have broken Christ's heart, but he did not bankrupt His mercy! Christ does not embarrass him before the others. He does not treat him with contempt but with utmost courtesy. All of them ate; all of them drank. Christ respected Judas' freedom to betray as He did Peter's freedom to deny, all without judgment. They judged themselves.

The Garden

When Judas betrayed Jesus in the Garden, he identified Christ with a kiss—a familiar greeting. Jesus responded, *"Friend, why are you here?"* (Mt 26.50). When the guards took Jesus away, none of his disciples could be found. They had all fled. There is little resistance and Judas' agenda is up in flames.

When Christ is placed before the Sanhedrin, they try to bring false testimony against Him. They find none, not even Judas (Mt 26.59). Then the claim Jesus made about destroying the Temple and his blasphemy saying, "He was God," was brought out in the open. He was judged guilty and deemed worthy of death (Mt 26.66).

Judas watched the entire affair. When He saw that Jesus was condemned to death, he took action (Mt 27.3-5). Judas was remorseful and repented by saying, "I have sinned in betraying innocent blood." However, He had served their purpose and he throws the money down and leaves. Judas' mind convicted him of right from wrong and he went out and hanged himself—could it have been an honourable suicide, understanding "an eye for an eye?"

The Lessons of Judas

Judas is definitely not far removed from any one of us! He is not an anonymous element within the church of Jesus Christ. The possibilities of becoming a Judas lie within everyone as a portrait of sin and betrayal, but it is also a wonderful cameo of His grace.

All of us have the potential of placing our own agenda and plans far above God's purposes. When we do this, we betray His intentions for our lives. Our lives are not set on "automatic pilot!" And virtue is never guaranteed. Each one of us has a price where we can be bought, compromising our faith. But, our darkness is vincible. No sin is unforgivable.

> *Judas is definitely not far removed from any one of us!*

Every one of us are capable of holding back from any kind of radical commitment to the person and plan of Christ. Therefore, our lives must change significantly, our priorities must shift, and our values must be reviewed in living out God's purpose. Judas missed so much because he was looking for something else.

God will never force us to be faithful. Judas is not the only one who attends the Lord's Supper and then goes out and denies or betrays the Lord. We eat the

Lord's supper not only to gain the power to say "No!" to sin, but also to acknowledge our sinful capability and allow His love to conquer.

Judas did not just sin. He sinned, and then realized his sin. Our sin is not the ultimate thing that can happen to us. Grace is. Judas grieved before he took his life. His betrayal of Christ did not mean Christ rejected him. Jesus loved Judas as much after he sinned as before he did. It is never too late to say, *"Lord, forgive me!"* The key here is this: God does not predestine us to sin against His will—we choose to sin!

> **Decision determines destiny.**

Life Purpose

Chapter 12
Knowledge of Divine Intention

"You only live once, but if you work it right, once will be enough!"
Joe Lewis—*World Boxing Champion*

Once Christopher Columbus was invited to abanquet where he was assigned the most honourableplace at the table. A shallow courtier who was meanly jealous of him asked him abruptly, "Had you not discovered the Indies, are there not other men in Spain who would have been capable of the same enterprise? Columbus made no reply but took an egg and invited the company of men to make it stand on end. They all attempted,but in vain, whereupon he tapped it on the table, denting one end and left it standing. "We all could have done it that way!" the courtier accused."Yes, if you had only known how," retortedColumbus. "And once I showed you the way to the New World, all you had to do was follow."

Author Unknown

Critical to pursuing God's purpose and plans and the discovery of our own personal destiny is what I call the *"knowledge of intention."* Whatever God does, He does intentionally and with purpose. It is very important we fully understand that His intention is very broadly based and universally established as a principle of creation.

All of creation displays God's intention and purpose. The incredible truth connected to that assertion is that creation innately knows the reason or purpose for its existence and functions accordingly.

Let's take a closer look at this claim and see if it bears up under scrutiny.

The universe operates by divine law and functions according to its charted courses. There is a "course" to nature (Jas 3.6). God created the universe (Ge 1) and is even now "upholding all things by the power of His word" (Heb 1.3, KJV). The laws of the universe govern everything from the orbits of the celestial heavens to the gravitational pull we experience on earth.

> **Creation innately knows the reason for its existence.**

From the make-up of the smallest atom to the revolution of the largest star, everything in the universe yields itself to the will and purpose of God. Solomon, looking at the monotony of nature, declared in Ecclesiastes:

> "The sun also rises and the sun goes down, and hastens to the place where it rises. The wind goes to the south, and circles about to the

Life Purpose

north; it circles and circles about continually, and on its circlings the wind returns again. All the rivers run into the sea, yet the sea is not full (1.5-7, AMP)."

It is little wonder Solomon is known for his wisdom.

The sun can be trusted to "rise again!" The moon can be depended upon to show herself at dusk. The waters of the ocean cycle to the sky and rain on the earth again. The law of gravity guarantees our safety. The law of aerodynamics enables us to safely predict the possibility of flight. The sun, moon, stars, and earth do not have a brain to instinctively know what God's intention is for their existence. However, they follow their orbital patterns. They yield to their distances and submit to continuous patterns of faithful function. They do not break from the spoken word of God. They seem to know what to do and when to obey. Yet, they are inanimate creations.

Hebrews 11.3 declares that it is "by faith we understand that the worlds [during the successive ages] were framed (fashioned, put in order, and equipped for their intended purpose) by the Word of God, so that what we see was not made out of things which are visible."

The *plant* kingdom operates under submission to the will and Word of God. In Genesis 1.11 God said, "Let the earth put forth (tender) vegetation; plants yielding seed, and the fruit trees yielding fruit each according to its kind, whose seed is in itself upon the earth. And it was so" (AMP).

Science can study this phenomena, replicate it, and copy it, but they cannot create it. What a wonderful security the farmer experiences, knowing that he can trust God's law written into the genetic codes of plant life. What mass confusion would there be if plant regeneration, according to its kind, could not be trusted! The farmer would plant rice and see the emergence of mango orchards, plant carrots and reap pumpkins.

Last time I checked, the plant kingdom did not have a brain so that it could understand its purpose and abide by the Word of God. Yet somehow the little watermelon seed knows what it will be when it grows up and proceeds on its course, reproducing after itself, until it reaches full maturity.

And talk about potential and destiny? One can count the number of seeds in an apple, but one will never be able to count the number of apples in one seed. When the seed yields to the Creator's intention, its life is maximized beyond belief. We can learn a great deal from the faithfulness of the seed that gives itself to the ground for our sake.

The *fish* kingdom is another aspect of God's creation that reflects intention. I live on the Pacific side of Canada and have had the opportunity to fish for the much prized Coho and Spring salmon. The life story of the salmon is a prime example of one part of God's creation fulfilling its life purpose and destiny.

Life Purpose

> Science can study this phenomena, replicate it, and copy it, but they cannot create it.

The salmon spawn in a stream located somewhere in the Pacific mountain regions and make their way down their birth stream into the British Columbian rivers, then out to sea. Here they make a profound shift in their living environment, from fresh water to salt water. They holiday in the Pacific for about four years, and then, by some inbuilt mechanism, follow their path back to reproduce and die in the very same river and stream that birthed them.

Thus the salmon lives and dies without the use of maps, compass, watches, Palm Pilots, cell phones, or even satellite location systems. Amazing inner technology placed within them by their Creator gets them to their destination and back again, and on time. Humanity gets lost in the shopping malls and would still be in the maze if it were not for information booths with people and maps reminding them, *"You are here."* Then we try to locate our car in the parking lot! That is enough to convince me there's a God!

Once again, the salmon has limited brain power and no spiritual capability to relate to God. Yet, the salmon knows what it is, what it is to do, where to go, and how to return to its place of origin within a very specific time period.

The *bird* kingdom also demonstrates the knowledge of intention. Jeremiah 8.7 states:

"[Even the migratory birds are punctual to their seasons.] Yes, the stork (excelling in the great height of her flight) in the heavens knows her appointed times of migration. And the turtledove, the swallow and the crane observe the time of their return; but my people do not know the law of the Lord [which the lower animals instinctively recognize in so far as it applies to them] (AMP)."

In Canada, we have the Canadian geese. What an awesome sight and sound to behold as they pass overhead, going south for the winter: focused on a destination that is sometimes thousands of miles away. You see their V formation and you hear their honking as they keep each other in line, gracefully streamlining their position in flight to maximize their strength for the journey. After winter has passed (whew!), you hear them honking as they return to the same fields they had left.

If the question hasn't emerged out of your heart yet, let me ask it for you: *"What or who tells them it is time to leave, and what or who tells them it is time to return?"* Maybe they can hear the weather reports or understand our weather channels. Maybe they e-mail each other to let one another know that it is springtime in Canada and the snow has melted, that it is safe to return home.

All I know is this. The Canadian goose is much smarter than most Canadians. At least they know when it is time to leave the cold and head south for

Life Purpose

a holiday to enjoy some warmth. Most of us stay in Canada and freeze while the Canadian goose, a big duck, is taking in the sun in Mexico! Go figure!

The *animal* kingdom affirms the knowledge of intention. I have always been an avid student of nature. I love to take my 1978 Toyota Land Cruiser ("The Green Machine") into the local mountains, going where few have gone before, and observe the animals that inhabit the area. Only one afternoon on a mountainside confirms to my heart the incredible instinct that guides the animal's every move.

> **We stay in Canada and freeze while the Canadian goose, a big duck, is taking in the sun in Mexico. Just Go figure!**

Instinctively, the animal kingdom expresses divine intention. They know what to do, what to eat, where to bed down, when to mate, how to defend themselves, how to prepare for winter, how to survive predators. I have had the privilege of observing the very powerful grizzly bear, the majestic elk, the lumbering moose, the fleeting deer, the gait of the wolf: every type of animal, from birth on, instinctively knows how it must behave to live and survive in the great Canadian outdoors.

The Human Factor

That leaves us to evaluate the knowledge of intention in man. Did God create the universe with a sense of purpose and leave man, the height of all creation, devoid of ability to know and do what he was created for? I don't believe so, but let's evaluate the evidence and draw conclusions from the Word.

Creation

When God created man, He also gave him a very similar sense of identity, purpose, and destiny. Genesis 1–3 reveals a number of important details about man's creation. Let's look at some of these similarities.

- *Man was made in the image of God, after God's likeness—to display His nature and character on earth (1.26);*
- *Man was given authority to subdue the rest of creation, to bring it under His control and influence, and to give everything a name—man was created to exhibit God's power and authority in the earth (1.26; 2.20);*
- *Man was given the presence of God—he was created to know God intimately, Spirit to spirit, and to express His presence on earth (3.8);*
- *Man was given prosperity, supernatural resources so there would be no physical need (1.29; 2.9);*
- *Man was given purpose, a sense of mission—God created man to be fruitful, multiply, fill the earth, and subdue it; using its resources for the service of God and man.*

Fall

We know that a tragedy took place in this scenario. The Bible records it in Genesis 3. Man and woman sinned against their Creator, disrespected His mandate, disobeyed His Word, and yielded to the influence of one whose intention was to destroy life. In defying God's authority, his own authority to operate was undermined. His loss was unimaginable.

- The image of God was lost—man is no longer created in the image of God, but creates after himself, after a fallen image marred by sin (Ge 5.1-3);
- The authority to operate as a representative of God was lost—man no longer could operate in dominion over, but became a servant to satan and sin (Lk 4.6; Ro 3);
- The presence of God was lost to Adam and Eve and they were expelled from the Garden of Eden—man no longer experienced intimacy. Sin changed all that (Ge 3.8, 24);
- Prosperity was removed from them—man now had to fight the rest of creation to provide for his physical needs to live. He now earned the right to live by the sweat of his brow (Ge 3.17-19);
- Their life purpose was lost—mankind now struggled for his existence, fighting the elements without and a fallen nature within (Ge 4.7).

Sin robs.

Sin robbed man of physical strength (Ge 3.3) and emotional health, experiencing emotions they had not known before—shame (3.7), guilt (hid themselves—3.8), fear (3.10). Sin robbed them of their mental clarity, causing them to blame others for their own sin and not accept responsibility for their personal actions (3.12-13). Sin robbed them of their spiritual life and relationship to God (3.22). Sin also destroyed their capability of provision, causing them to fight for everything they got (3.16-19).

Sin affected man's sense of identity, who he was. It also affected his sense of purpose, what he was supposed to do. Sin affected man's destiny, where God was trying to take him. Man has desperately struggled from that point, to this, with these questions: "Who am I? Why am I here? What am I supposed to do? Where am I going?"

Recreation

Christ came as a solution to man's tragic situation. Because of a revitalized relationship to God through Jesus, obedience to the Word of God, and being born into the family of God, what was taken away from us is returned to us.

- Godly character and nature is restored to us at salvation. We are "recreated in the image of God" (Eph 4.23-24);

- Authority to act as a representative of God is restored (Eph 1.18-23);
- Presence is restored—man is reconciled to God through Christ (2Co 5.16-19);
- Prosperity and provision is restored (Mt 6.33; 2Co 9.8-10);
- Purpose is restored.

"For we are God's very [own] handiwork (His workmanship), recreated in Christ Jesus, [born anew] that we may do those good works which God predestined (planned beforehand) for us, (taking paths which he prepared ahead of time) that we should walk in them—living the good life which He pre-arranged and made ready for us to live" (Eph. 2.10, AMP).

Man, without a revelation of purpose that comes only through a relationship to Jesus Christ, is the only aspect of all of creation that does not know instinctively his reason for life, or his own knowledge of divine intention. He struggles to know what all of creation innately understands. This is found in every culture and in every nation.

This issue puzzled me for many years. I asked the Lord why this confusion exists in the human heart. I understood the block that sin made, but I did not have the clarity I needed on the issue. God spoke to me one day and said this, succinctly and simply: *"I have withheld a knowledge of purpose so that man would seek Me."*

God desires relationship with us. The Bible makes it clear that "He knows the thoughts and the plans that He has for us, plans to prosper us and not to harm us, to give us a hope and a future" (Jer 29.11). When man pursues God and seeks him with all his heart, He unveils the mystery of His will and shows man where he fits in the divine scheme of things. However, there will be an uneasy silence for those who refuse to seek Him. It is mandatory that you make the right choice.

> ***It matters who you marry.***

The Extension of Divine Intention

If God knows by heart the purpose He has for human life, it naturally fits there is a purpose for the extension of human life into every aspect of society. It is critical we do not think solely in terms of our own personal mission and call, but that we understand the entire corporate nature of divine intention. Let's look at a few of these natural extensions of personal purpose.

Marriage—Marriage is God-ordained: it is an ordinance of the Church, meaning, it must occur under the "orders" of God. Marrying outside of His permission will complicate your life. It matters who you marry. "What has a believer in common with an unbeliever? What agreement [can there be between]

Life Purpose

a temple of God and idols? For we are the temple of the living God" (2Co 6.15-16, AMP). Amos said, "How can two walk together unless they be in agreement?" (Am 3.3). Marrying *"outside"* of God's will can have some extremely tragic consequences and lead a person to compromise on the call. Marrying *"within"* the context of God's will opens the door for two people to interconnect their destinies and fulfill together what they could not possibly have fulfilled alone. As the minister asserts: "What God has joined together, let no man tear asunder!"

When a couple desire to wed, it is critical they be asked about their sense of mission and calling in life. How can a young man ask a woman to marry and go with him? The sense of calling and purpose resting on each person should be shared and evaluated as to whether or not they are travelling in the same direction. If not, someone's call will be compromised.

I believe there is destiny that rests upon marriages. Couples need a prophetic sense about their coming together. They need to seek God as to their corporate purpose. Without it, the marriage will deteriorate: "Without a vision, the people perish" (Pr 29.18). One translation says they "live carelessly!" From my pastoral point of view a couple that does not have a clear purpose for their marriage will see marital breakdown, and the motivation to stay together will diminish.

Family—fatherhood and family was established by the Father of all fathers (Eph 3.15). It was His idea.

He formed it on purpose. He gave it order (1Co 11.3; Eph 5.21-33). His desire is to see a holy seed emerge from righteous relationships (Mal 2.15). The family is the most basic building block of society. The Church, the community, and the nation is only as healthy as the natural family.

Every family has a life purpose. They experience family assignments and carry a special anointing and calling. Unique gifts are in their possession for the Kingdom's use and for His glory. Every family is known for its vices (such as the Mafia and their criminal activity) or for its virtues (for example, Reverend Billy Graham and world evangelism, salvation).

I am blessed to have both my father, Arnold Kalamen and my son, Brodie Kalamen serving on my pastoral team at Kelowna Christian Center. It was a rare honor for us to stand together one Father's Day and tag-team the preaching of the Word from the perspective of three generations of pastors.

History is replete with illustrations of third generation spiritual apathy. A case could be made of families becoming progressively weaker and weaker in their spiritual experience from generation to generation. An entire book of the Bible, Judges, illustrates that potentiality. However, God spoke to me one day and said that the "anointing resting upon our family would increase until the brightness of noon day sun" (Pr 4.18).

I remind my children that they are upholding the name of Christ with their righteous talk and

Life Purpose

behaviour, ensuring that the Kalamen name is honoured throughout the generations. When people think about our family, I want them to think of the passion our family had for missions, financing and building the kingdom, and leading God's people into God's best. I want our family to stand for something: when all is said and done, I want us to have said and done what God intended us to do.

> **God reminds us that our children are "arrows in the bow of a warrior."**

God reminds us that our children are "arrows in the bow of a warrior" (Ps 127.4). As a holy warrior, I want to draw back God's bow and help to direct my children towards the target. I desire them to hit the center of God's will for their lives. I want them to do damage to the enemy's kingdom in the Name of Jesus Christ.

Generations—in Isaiah 41.4, the prophet writes:

> "Who has prepared and done this, calling and guiding the destinies of the generations of the nations from the beginning? I, the Lord—the first [existing before history began] and with the last [an everpresent, unchanging God]; I am He!" (AMP).

Each and every generation has a divine intention to live out. It is the responsibility of every generation to locate God's will and serve His purposes in their generation, like it was reported King David did (Ac 13.22, 36). Every generation carries a unique anointing to bring the message of Christ: it is the same message, but with different methods.

I encountered God through the Jesus Movement when I was attending Southern California College in Costa Mesa, California. It was my generation who founded the songs, the methodology, the heart to affect their peers with the Gospel. Many men and women in the ministry today came out of, or were profoundly affected by the Jesus Movement of those days.

This generation is different from my own generation. This generation is the *"chosen generation"* (1Pe 2.9) God has raised up to influence and reach out to millions of young people who are in desperate need of a message of hope. Each generation has to respond to the call. Somebody will influence this now generation and it, too, will be known for its vices or virtues.

The Church, local churches, and denominations— God has raised up denominations and local churches with very specific commissions, callings, and mandates for world impact. God has a purpose for His Church and only works through His Church to implement divine strategy.

Listen to the Apostle Paul's exhortation to the church in Ephesians 3.8-11:

> "Although I am less than the least of all God's people, this grace was given me: to preach

Life Purpose

to the Gentiles the unsearchable riches of Christ, and to make plain to everyone the administration of this mystery, which for ages past was kept hidden in God, who created all things. His intent was that now, through the Church, the manifold wisdom of God should be made known to the rulers and authorities in the heavenly realms, according to His eternal purpose which He accomplished in Christ Jesus our Lord."

> ***I love the Church. I love God's people. I love the Body of Christ.***

I love the Church. I love God's people. I love the Body of Christ. The Apostle Paul firmly states that the Church is a corporate thing. God is keenly interested in kingdom impact. He speaks about it as a "manifold wisdom!" When the Body of Christ is properly assembled, a manifold wisdom is expressed. What God was planning behind the scenes, in secret, what was beyond finding out (Greek anexichniaston—unsearchable) will be openly shown in the light to every one: not only will humanity marvel at His wisdom, the heavenly beings—demons and angels—will talk about it and know its authority! "Principalities (Greek archais) and also powers (Greek exousia)" will "know" the Church, both earthly and heavenly. Paul reminds us that God has an eternal purpose.

It is key that denominations, men of God, and local churches be brought into alignment with their personal and corporate prophetic destiny. The degree to how successful we are in helping to clarify and establish the five-fold ministry's prophetic destiny and the degree to which we are successful in helping local churches see their place, it will be to that degree that we will see how or if the present-day Church and kingdom generation fulfill its corporate prophetic destiny.

When individuals, local churches, or denominations forget their prophetic assignment and purpose for existence, they risk losing their mandate and being replaced. They perish without a prophetic revelation of their commission. When a local church was birthed by God with intention, as it fully submits to fulfilling that intention, there is blessing. When we operate outside of God's mandate, it is like moving outside the metron of spiritual influence that Paul needed to be honoured in 2 Corinthians 10.14.

Denominations and churches must celebrate the different mandates resting upon each assembling of people. There are many different purposes resting on different churches. Different messages are required of different faith communities. It is crucial that we see each other's role in the Kingdom and co-operate rather than compete. Everyone is needed if the objective of city and world impact is going to be released. The Church needs to be a radical agent that produces a righteous counter-culture to the world system.

Cities—throughout scripture God sent prophets and apostles to cities with a message of mercy and/or judgment. Most of those encounters were calls for

Life Purpose

cities to return to God's original intention and align themselves to God's purpose.

There has been much written in the Christian community about taking cities for God and rebuilding the devastation of generations (Isa 61.1-4). Some of the most influential Christian videos in recent years have been associated with Community Transformation. Wonderful testimonies of God's miraculous intervention in city after city are now emerging from all around the world. Cities are like corporate personalities. They carry a reason for existence.

Some cities were founded by righteous people, and some cities were founded by people with evil intent. A city is known by either its sin or its righteousness: for example, Amsterdam (prostitution and drugs), San Francisco (homosexuality), Las Vegas (gambling), Paris (fashion design), and Bangkok (child prostitution), Colorado Springs (a home base for many Christian organizations). I could go on.

"Fruitful in Unity."

I live in the city of Kelowna which is located in the very beautiful province of British Columbia, Canada. This region is called the Okanagan Valley and is known for its wide variety of orchards and vineyards. The founding fathers of our city appropriately named its motto: "Fruitful in Unity!" This call to unity is part of our spiritual and corporate DNA. To despise that call is to see the city depart from God's original intention and open its gates to all kinds of evil.

What do you want your city to be known for? Research the origins of your city and do an in-depth evaluation of it. Then consider the primary causes for its being and any prophetic words concerning why it exists. How can a city be called to repentance if it does not know what to repent from and what it is to become? Cities are waiting to be redeemed to God's original intention. It is going to take a bold company of discerners, intercessors, prophets, and those with an apostolic authority to awaken a city to its sin, its calling, and corporate purpose. Find out what purpose God has for your city or town.

Nations—in Acts 17 we read of Paul's discourse with the philosophers of Athens, both religious and non-religious. In his discussions with these learned men of his day, he makes this very profound statement:

> "And He made from one [common origin, one source, one blood] all nations of men to settle on the face of the earth, having definitely determined [their] allotted periods of time and the fixed boundaries of their habitations—so that they should seek God, in the hope that they might feel after Him and find Him, although he is not far from each one of us. For in Him we live and move and have our being (verses 26-28, AMP)."

God miraculously raises up one nation and brings down another. He uses nations for His purposes as He did Babylon for Israel (Isa 14.24-27). He has a

Life Purpose

plan for people groups, a plan for their salvation, just as he did for Israel (Jer 29.10-14): the Israelites lost connection to their purposes in Babylon, but God had not forgotten them and would bring them back to their own land after seventy years of captivity was complete. God establishes the borders of nations (Isa 26.13-15).

I remember ministering at a YWAM Taiwan conference in the early 1990s. The Christian community was shaken by recent prophetic words concerning a potential outbreak of war between China and Taiwan. It was troubling to watch many thousands of Christians flee the island. When I went into prayer, I asked the Lord for an understanding of why this occurred. God made the history clear to me, reminding me that Taiwan had become the storehouse for much of the wealth of China when leaders fled communism. The political leaders had thought of re-invasion and needed the wealth to do so.

God said to me, "I have brought the wealth to the island so that the Christian community would re-invade mainland China, spiritually, with the resources I have permitted them to have. If they don't use their resources for Kingdom purposes, they will lose their resources."

Not too long ago Canada was facing a critical vote in Quebec concerning separation from Confederation. I had been asked to speak at a minister's conference in Ottawa just prior to the vote, called together to intercede for God's intervention. *I spoke on*

Reconciling Canada to the Purposes of God.

The message was simple. Look at the prophetic lineage and the words God has spoken over Canada through the founding fathers. One specific word emerged: the Dominion of Canada was to be a nation under God "from sea to sea" (Sir Samuel Leonard Tilley, from his prayer journal on Psalm 72.8).

Intercession must have a fixed focus and it must be to pray according to the will of God. We prayed His will be done, as He had purposed it to be, and we fought together for Canada's redemptive purpose to come to pass. A vote to separate was defeated—Canada remains together, from sea to sea.

> **If they don't use their resources for Kingdom purposes, they will lose their resources.**

God has an intention for the universe, man—you and I, our marriages, families, generations, the Church, cities, and nations. Understanding that intention, connecting in prayer to His plan and purposes, and working on fulfilling His will is one of the greatest joys of life. God desires us to be history makers, living our lives in conjunction with His Story.

> **"Purposes, like eggs, unless they be hatched into action, will run into rottenness."**
> Samuel Smiles

Life Purpose

Chapter 13
I Did It On Purpose

When Michelangelo was preparing to sculpt the figure David, he first studied the character of the brave young shepherd boy. The artist began by asking himself: "When did David achieve greatness? Was it when he killed Goliath? Or when he decided to do it?" He concluded that it was the decision and not the slaying that made David a giant in his own right.

Francis Gay, *The Friendship Book* (1985)

"There is one quality more important than know-how. That is know-how by which we determine not only to accomplish our purpose, but what our purpose is to be."

Norber Wiener, *Scientist*

How passionate are you to see God's purpose and plan come to fruition in your life? How aggressively are you pursuing His will for your life? And just how desperate are you to locate your life purpose in Christ? Are you "pressing towards the goal to win the prize to which Christ Jesus is calling you?" (Php 3.12).

> **This violence is similar to the aggressiveness of a baby in the birth canal.**

You will never see your full potential maximized until you grab hold of destiny in your heart. You will never become the you God intended until you get serious about knowing Him and knowing His will. Jesus said, "the violent take the kingdom by force" (Mt 11.12). This violence is similar to the aggressiveness of a baby in the birth canal. It has to push forward in order to have new life. If you want to find a life that gives significance, you have got to mean business about serving the purposes of God in this generation and get your priorities in line.

The Principle of Incarnation

"It was God (personally present) in Christ, reconciling and restoring the world to favour with Himself."
2 Corinthians 5.19a, *Amplified*

"And the Word [Christ] became flesh (human, incarnate) and tabernacled—fixed His tent of flesh, lived awhile—among us."
John 1.14a, *Amplified*

The Incarnation of Christ (Latin "in" and caro, "flesh"), the act of God assuming flesh, is one of the most discussed doctrines in the entire history of Christendom. Lewis Sperry Chafer places the incarnation as one of the seven greatest events that have ever occurred in the history of the universe (*Systematic Theology* [1948], 7.194). That God, through His Son, would have ever considered identifying Himself so completely with the human race is an event of immeasurable importance.

The principle of incarnation is deeply woven into the very fabric of everything that God does: for example, "the principle of God always moving through human flesh, via human instrumentality." What He did through His Son, He wants to do through us. He wants to break into our souls, break through to our heart, and break out in His love to serve a generation through us. He wants to do the same things through us that He did through His Son, Jesus, when he walked on planet earth.

You Can Know the Plan Personally

God said, "I know the thoughts and the plans that I have for you, plans to prosper you and not harm you, to give you a hope and a future" (Jer 29.11). The Apostle Paul wrote that we are God's workmanship, recreated in Christ to do good works which God planned beforehand (Eph 2.10). We must get to know what good works He has planned for us to do.

The Apostle Paul expressed this thought to the Philippian church: "God, who began a good work in you, will continue developing [that good work] and perfecting and bringing it to completion in you"

(Php 1.6). We need to trust that God is not only the Author of our faith, but the Finisher of it as well (Heb 12.2). King David understood that and said, "the Lord would perfect that which concerned [him]" (Ps 138.8). Believe with me that God will work with us until what He has deposited within us emerges for the good of a generation.

We can know God's plan for our life in several ways:

By creation—at birth, many people have had their sense of mission verbalized: for instance, *John the Baptist* (Mt 3.1-3); *Isaiah* (44.2); *Jeremiah* (1.5). Even Paul alludes to this calling from the womb, though this event preceded his salvation and receiving a heavenly commissioning for his life (Gal 1.15).

By salvation—I have recognized this fact, over and over again, that at an individual's conversion there is a dream seed placed in their heart about their mission in life. The Apostle Paul, in Acts 9, received a heavenly vision concerning his life purpose. God affirmed this calling: "This man is a chosen instrument of Mine to bear My name before the Gentiles and kings and the descendants of Israel; for I will make it clear to him how much he will be afflicted and must endure for My name's sake" (verses 15-16).

> **Destiny is not decided, but discovered.**

God promises to make our calling clear to us. The rest is entirely up to us. From Paul's own lips, we read that he believed he had not been "disobedient

Life Purpose

to the heavenly vision" (Ac 26.16-19). Tragically, it is possible to have a clear mission and mandate from Heaven and disobey or disregard it.

By revelation—destiny is not decided, but discovered. For many of us, knowing His will can be a long-term process. At some point the dots of God's dealings and leadings in our life are connected and life takes on significance and meaning. Like Queen Esther, we discover why we were brought into the Kingdom for such a day as this.

The Apostle Paul continually invested this scripture into the life of the church:

> "[For I always pray] that He would grant you a spirit of wisdom and revelation in the [deep and intimate] knowledge of [God], by having the eyes of your heart flooded with light, so that you can know and understand the hope to which he has called you and how rich is His glorious inheritance in the saints [you and I]—His set-apart ones" (Eph 1.17-18)."

God wants us to know the hope of our calling. He wants us to have spiritual insight into His plans and where we fit in the scheme of things.

"Until your desire to become you matches God's desire for you to become you, you will never become you."
Andrew Shearman

Chapter 14

Marching Orders

"When marching orders have been given, it is a sin to stand at attention."

David Kalamen

During the reign of Oliver Cromwell, the British government began to run low on silver for coins. Lord Cromwell sent his men on an investigation of the local cathedrals to see if they would find any precious metal there. After investigating, they reported: "The only silver we could find is the statues of the saints standing in the corners." To which the radical soldier and statesman of England replied: "Good! We'll melt down the saints and put them into circulation."

Chuck Swindoll, *Come Before Winter* (page 45)

 The thoughts and plans God has for our lives are always in conjunction with something else that God is wanting to do. God calls us to participate with Him in the unfolding of human history. I call them personal calls, assignments, or orders from heaven. They begin as small requests; but I guarantee they will graduate

Life Purpose

into larger requests. When we are "faithful in the little things" (Lk 16.10), God can trust us with the bigger things of the Kingdom.

These heavenly orders come in the form of *daily, seasonal,* and *life* assignments. In my personal life, I have always been amazed at the detailed manner in which God speaks to me and at the clarity of His divine commissioning of my life. Being a member of God's squad and receiving an assignment from Him is one of the greatest privileges I have had, and I have observed that every act of my obedience to the assignments that He has given me has paved the way for greater responsibility and authority. Are you ready to receive His marching orders?

> ***Every day is an adventure for a purpose-led Christian.***

Daily Assignments

Every day is an adventure for a purpose-led Christian. Their hearts are open to hearing the Word of God and their spirit is open to listening to His voice. There is nothing in the world that comes even close to being used by God. Once you have experienced being "led by the Spirit" (Ro 8.14), you never want to go back to just mundane living.

The Father is always at work. Just as He assigned His Son walking orders for the day, He wants His children to receive Kingdom work on a daily basis. I am convinced that many opportunities for divine action pass by a large percentage of Christians every day. God wants all His people activated and energized for the work ahead of them. He wants them paying close attention to His leading and follow Him.

Ananias

One of the most specific and detailed daily assignments I know of in scripture is found in Acts 9. It is the story of a disciple named Ananias impacting the life of a new convert to the faith, Saul of Tarsus. When you read through this particular portion of scripture, you can only be impressed by the clarity of the directives that he received.

Let me fill you in on some history behind the story. Saul was an appointed and authorized religious authority, sent out by the Jews to imprison all who called themselves Christians. On the road to Damascus, Saul encounters the Lord Jesus Christ. He is physically blinded by the encounter, though his spiritual eyes had been opened up.

Ananias is a disciple, a disciplined one. A disciple is one who hears the Word and acts on the Word he hears (Jn 8.31-32). The Lord appears to Ananias in a vision: he answers, "Here I am, Lord!" He recognizes that it is his Lord speaking. The Lord then gives him very clear directions for the day. Get up—a good place to start. Don't stay in bed when God is saying "get up!"

Life Purpose

- Go to the street called Straight—assignments always have a go aspect to them; you cannot stay where you are and go on with God; you have to make a decision.
- Ask at the house of Judas—a specific house.
- Ask for a man from Tarsus called Saul.
- He is praying.
- He has seen a man called Ananias lay hands on him.
- His eyesight will be healed.

You may say, "If I had directions like that, I would get up and go too!" However, many of us could get clear directions like that if we were really listening and desiring God to use us. It is my observation that many of us get similar leadings and wiggle our way out of acting on them somehow. We explain the leadings away. And then we wait and wait and wait for continuous clarification and confirmation. We back off because of fear. We pass the buck to someone else.

> **Assignments always have a go aspect to them.**

Ananias began to do just that. "Lord, I have heard many people talk about this man, especially what evil and great suffering he has brought on Your saints." But, the Lord said, *"Go!"* I can hear Ananias trying to mentally argue with God and figure it all out for himself: *"You want me to go, reveal my Christian identity, and after that volunteer for prison duty?"* But (not butt), Ananias obeyed the word of the

Lord. This is the first step towards receiving another assignment!

If you could jump between the lines of scripture and use your righteous imagination for a moment, you would see Ananias gingerly checking on the Damascus city map for a street called Straight. Maybe it won't be there!

- He finds the street: confirmation #1.
- He goes to the street and asks if there is a man named Judas who lives on the street: he does—confirmation #2.
- He asked Judas if there is a Saul from Tarsus inside: there is—confirmation #3.
- He asks if this Saul is blind: he is—confirmation #4.
- He asks if Saul is expecting anyone and whether Saul knows the name of the person: he is, and he does, because God has started training a disciple and a young convert with clear vision—confirmation #5.

Do you think it was difficult for Ananias to presuppose he could lay his hands upon Saul, pray boldly for healing of his eyes, and believe with all confidence that a miracle would take place? I am fully persuaded these many confirmations released a large measure of faith in Ananias, and he believed that the supernatural power of God would manifest on Saul's behalf. And, it did—Saul arose and he was baptized.

Life Purpose

What do you think dinner time with the family was like in Ananias' home or, when church opened for meetings, who do you think was the first one to grab a microphone and start sharing a testimony about God's activity in his life? Do you think Ananias "reported for duty" the following day? I believe he did. Ananias was a key player in bringing one of the most effective apostles who ever lived into the kingdom. One can only ponder what might not have been had Ananias not been obedient to the voice of the Lord.

Daily assignments should be a routine expectation for the Christian. Christ prayed and daily received His heavenly orders. As believers, we ought to develop a prayer routine and receive His heavenly orders for the day; thereby, creating a keen sensitivity in our spirit for supernatural activity. Our lives ought to be like a "vessel set apart and useful for honourable and noble purposes, consecrated and profitable to the Master, fit and ready for any good work" (2Ti 2.21, AMP).

Scripture is replete with illustrations of daily assignments. Each one of them carries an incredible testimony to the clarity of God's directions. The Book of the Acts of the Apostles is a tremendous encouragement for all of us concerning God's people honouring heavenly assignments.

Acts 10 speaks about Peter's encounter with Cornelius who was visited by an angel. Cornelius was informed:

> "Send men to Joppa, and have them call for and invite here a certain Simon whose

surname is Peter; he is lodging with Simon a tanner, whose house is by the seaside. Just as they were approaching town, Peter went up to the roof of the house to pray. He saw a vision. While Peter was earnestly trying to resolve the vision in His mind, the Holy Spirit said to him, 'Behold, three men are looking for you! Get up and go downstairs and go with them, without hesitation, for I have sent them.'"

> **Daily assignments should be a routine expectation for the Christian.**

Do you see the similarities? God's assignments are very clear. The critical part is not the vision, the angel, or the voice of the Holy Spirit, but the actions of personal obedience. Reject the directive and heaven may be silent for awhile because we have despised His call. Respond to the directive and our lives may never be the same again.

In Acts 11.25-26 we read of Barnabas, a really good man, controlled by the Holy Spirit, and full of faith. He discerns a leading to "go to Tarsus and hunt for Saul." I am so grateful for this man reconnecting Saul to Kingdom business. Scripture says, "when he had found him, he brought him back to Antioch." It was not long after this that Saul received a divine commissioning for international evangelism (Ac 13.1-4).

I could go on. The point is clear: God wants to activate His people into participating with Him in

Life Purpose

bringing in the harvest and making history. God can do this today, through you, just as he did through men and women in times past.

"God Loves You and I Love You, Too!"

I was attending a minister's conference in Toronto not too many years ago. At break-time my wife and I decided to take a stroll through the shopping mall. When I entered a store, the Lord directed my attention to a young saleswoman behind the perfume counter and gave me an assignment: "Go and tell her that I love her and that you love her too!" My wife is a very understanding lady: she went and prayed, and I headed for the counter on a mission.

When I reached the counter, I said to the young lady: "Excuse me, I'm a Christian. God told me to tell you, 'God loves you' and, 'I love you, too!'" She absented herself from behind the counter in a burst of tears and ran out the back of the store. I was not sure what the Lord wanted me to do next, so prayerfully we began our walk back to the conference.

As I walked by a flower store the Lord said, "Buy the young lady one rose, put your card on it, and write: 'Remember, God loves you' and, 'I love you, too!'" I obeyed. I bought the rose and gave it to one of the employees to make sure the 'lady behind the counter' got the message.

A few weeks later I received a letter in the mail. In it was a description of this young lady's pain. She said she had been on a spiritual journey and had attended a church in Winnipeg for six weeks, but not one person had introduced themselves or shown her any love or interest. She left the church saying that God and Christians were liars.

That morning she cried out to God: "If you really exist, send someone to me today that will tell me that 'they' love me and that 'You' love me too!" I just happened to be the closest and available employee of God, and He gave me the job. She is now attending a church in downtown Toronto. That act of obedience opened my life to become a member of God's Squad and has given me many other opportunities to touch people's lives everywhere I go. What a privilege and a blessing to work for the King of Kings.

> *"To everything there is a season, and a time to every purpose under heaven."*
> Ecclesiastes 3.1

Seasonal Assignments

I love the natural seasons that exist in Canada. I appreciate the variety of colors and the differences in temperature. I love the challenge the cold weather brings. Canadians are constantly watching the weather. Seasons can descend upon them quickly. They have to be able to adapt fast and work with what the season brings. We found out early in life that you can't change the season when it is upon you: you have

Life Purpose

to change and reconcile yourself to the expectations of the season.

People go through seasons spiritually. Some heavenly assignments require a longer period of commitment to bring them to completion. It takes a willingness to last for the long haul. Words like perseverance, hard work, sacrifice, priorities, and time are associated with this kind of season. Like Rome, the assignment is not completed in a day: it requires a person who is willing to carry the responsibility until it's finished. So, follow the example of William Carey. When asked the reason for his success as a missionary, he replied, "I can plod."

People who are ready for seasonal assignments are not easy to find. They are a rare breed. But, we are assured that "God's eyes go to and fro throughout the whole world to show Himself strong on behalf of those who walk blamelessly before Him" (2Ch 16.9). He will find His man or woman who will bring to birth what is in His heart.

We find such a man in Nehemiah.

Nehemiah

Nehemiah first appears at Susa as cupbearer to King Artaxerxes (Ne 1.11–12.1) about 446 B.C. A cupbearer's job was to taste the king's wine: if he died, the king didn't drink it. Interesting job? He was risking his life for his king every day. He also sat in the king's presence when he was addressing the needs of the Persian empire.

One day he had visitors from his homeland, from the city of Jerusalem. He was informed of the deplorable conditions of his countrymen in Judea (read Lamentations), so Nehemiah set his heart to intercede for his nation. Prayer is a risky business. My experience with prayer is this: when I set myself to pray, God makes me part of the answer to my prayers. I am sure that is why many Christians do not pray as they should: if they pray, they will be hired from heaven and given an assignment.

Nehemiah 1 sheds light on the process that was behind the birthing of a seasonal assignment. There are some particular kinds of people that God is attracted to, giving them seasonal assignments to complete. Nehemiah fit the bill.

He made God's concerns his concerns. He committed himself to prayer and was willing to assume responsibility for the state of the nation. By doing this, he availed himself to obey God, regardless of the cost.

Three or four months later Nehemiah's request to the king, at the risk of his own life, was that he be allowed to go and rebuild Jerusalem—a city his masters had spent time and money destroying. His royal master granted his request and appointed him governor. God can do anything for a praying man or woman. Here, a cupbearer miraculously becomes the governor in a matter of moments. Nehemiah is connecting with his life purpose and destiny.

Accompanied by cavalry and letters from the king to the different governors through whose provinces

Life Purpose

he was to pass, as well as to Asaph, the keeper of the king's forests (he was to supply him with timber), he started on his journey, promising to return to Persia within a certain period of time (Neh 2.1-10).

> ***Nehemiah is a good example of someone who started with the end in mind.***

Without a moment's delay, Nehemiah began the task of restoring the city walls which was accomplished in the very short period of fifty-two days (Neh 6.15), 444 B.C. In this he was opposed by Sanballat and Tobiah who not only poured out a stream of abuse and contempt upon all who were engaged in the work, but actually made a conspiracy to fall upon the builders with an armed force and put a stop to the grandiose undertaking.

But Nehemiah managed to overcome all these obstacles with God's help. Besides rebuilding the walls, he reformed abuses, redressed grievances (Chapter 5), introduced law and order (Chapter 7), and revived worshiping God (Chapter 8). The people of Jerusalem had walked by the broken walls for years, but by the directive of God and a willing leader, the city was rebuilt. When that seasonal assignment was over and God's purpose was fulfilled, Nehemiah returned to serve his king at Susa. He truly is a good example of someone who started with the end in mind.

Nehemiah was used as a catalyst for restoring Jerusalem. Someone had to stand in the role of a mediator between the people and God and risk his life in carrying out and serving the purposes of God in his generation. Nehemiah surely overcame what all of us face:

- an identity crisis: "Who am I?"
- a rejection crisis: "What if they don't listen or believe me?"
- an inferiority crisis: "I don't have what it takes."
- a fear of failure crisis: "Send someone else."

Nehemiah broke through and completed the mission God had birthed in him through prayer. He didn't permit any kind of impossibilities to stop him. Who he knew God to be was greater than any opponents to the task. The Word of the Lord was greater than the opposition and words of men. He prayed, prepared a plan, and then worked the plan to its full completion. What an awesome testimony to a man and his God!

Life Assignments

I love it when a plan comes together. I love to see the end of a matter, not just its beginning. Such is the life of Joseph. Psalm 105.17-24 says, "He sent a man before them, even Joseph, who was sold for a servant: whose feet they hurt with fetters: he was laid in iron: until the time that his word came: the promise of the Lord tested him severely" (Har).

Life Purpose

Joseph, the Dreamer

Joseph is an excellent example of someone who persevered through an apparent contradiction of his faith. He was the eleventh son of Jacob. He became the ancestor of Israel's two northern tribes, Manasseh and Ephraim. Joseph was born in Padan-aram when his father was ninety years of age. He was his father's favourite son because of two things: he was the firstborn of Rachel; and, he was the son of his old age. His life story is covered in Genesis 37–50.

Joseph's propensity to supervise came early. At seventeen years of age he sends a "bad report back to his father" about his brothers. The favouritism created ill will between them. They hated him and could not even speak to him in peace. The clincher came when Joseph introduced two dreams to them: the first dream was about sheaves bowing; the second dream was about eleven stars, the sun, and the moon bowing. His family understood that both dreams portrayed his emergence as the leader of their family. His father rebuked him for the dreams but pondered them, for he himself had been a dreamer and dreams had led the entire family tree. But his brothers were jealous and angry and sought a way to end his life.

> ***I love it when a plan comes together.***

I believe God introduced Joseph to his life assignment when he was seventeen years old. Although he had a limited understanding of what his dreams meant, he never let go of them. Psalm 105 affirms this: "Until the time that his word came: the word of the Lord tested him" (NKJV, verse 19).

Psalm 12.6 says, "The words of the Lord are pure words; as silver tried in a furnace of earth, purified seven times" (KJV). Peter declared in 1 Peter 4.12: "Beloved, do not be amazed and bewildered at the fiery ordeal which is taking place to test your quality, as though something strange—unusual, and alien to you and your position—were befalling you" (AMP).

God was preparing a young man for his life assignment. He was going to use Joseph to transition a family to a clan, to a tribe, to a nation. Joseph was going to be a nation builder. God was raising him up to protect a family's development into a nation. There was really no better place for them to be than protected in the womb of the Egyptian empire: Israel would be protected by Pharaoh's power and then be released to grow within the secure borders of an Empire.

The Bible says that Joseph was "a man sent before them" (Ps 105.17). We must believe that what transpired in Joseph's life was totally permitted by God. Take a good look at some of these "fiery furnaces where the word of the Lord was refined!" I will refer to them as pits.

The Water Pit

The first pit Joseph was thrown into was a well. One day the brothers were in the fields and saw their brother, the dreamer, coming. At that moment they grabbed an opportunity to rid themselves of a family problem. They threw Joseph into a Coke bottle shaped well and left him to die. Only God knows what was going on in Joseph's mind, rejected by his brothers and hated enough to produce a murderous spirit. You must remember that the road to fulfilling your life purpose is not always paved with good intentions and the support of those closest to you.

The Slave Pit

Dead, Joseph was worth absolutely nothing. When his brothers saw an Ishmaelite caravan or slave traders, they decided to sell their brother into slavery for twenty pieces of silver. Why was it Joseph didn't die? Because the purposes of God had not been fulfilled: his destiny was just beginning. We are promised that the word of the Lord will not return void, but will accomplish that which God intends (Isa 55.11).

Joseph's apparent death broke the heart of his aged father, Jacob. His life was transformed in a matter of days from favourite son to rejected brother, from free man to slave. The pit carries a lot of different meanings to different people, but how does one escape them except "by the word of the Lord?" (see 1Co 10.13—"God is faithful").

David Kalamen

> *The road to fulfilling your life assignment is not always paved with good intentions and the support of those closest to you.*

The Snake Pit

Read Genesis 39. Joseph was bought by Potiphar, an officer of Pharaoh. Though he conducted himself with great integrity, trustworthiness, skill, and all that Potiphar had prospered, Joseph faced yet another challenge many of God's men have faced: sexual advances from Potiphar's wife. This story has a bit of a twist to it. My understanding of Egyptian culture established the woman as a great power and she was quite capable of divorcing one man and freeing another, so Joseph had a real temptation before him: possible freedom from a prison cell.

Her improper sexual advances towards Joseph created a crisis of conscience. Lesser men would have fallen. If Joseph yielded to her, his destiny would be affected. If he rejected her, he would have to face the consequences of a woman scorned. What protects any man or woman from compromising their destiny? I believe *"without a vision people perish"* (Pr 29.18). They dwell carelessly and fall into sin. Why? Because they do not believe sin will affect their life in any significant way.

However, God's dreamers and people who are walking in alignment to their sense of life purpose

Life Purpose

reject compromise. The price of missing God's will is too high. Joseph refused to go down that path, not because he was a better man than others, but because there was a calling on his life he did not want to violate. He believed the dream, so he said, *"How can I do this thing and sin against God?"* He was falsely accused of rape and thrown into another pit.

The Prison Pit

Though falsely accused, Joseph faces prison with an incredible strength and grace. His family may have deserted him, but the Bible says that "the Lord was with Joseph, and showed him mercy and gave him favour in the sight of the warden, and made whatever he did to prosper." How vital is keeping our integrity and the favour of the Lord when it comes to preserving our life purpose? Very!

Joseph demonstrates he did not give up his belief that his dreams were from the Lord. How? By the way he responds to answering the dreams of two of his other fellow prisoners (Genesis 40.8—"Do not interpretations belong to the Lord?"). The butler is restored; the baker was hung and beheaded. Joseph interprets those dreams with confidence. That is clear evidence his belief in dreams was solid. Later on, he responds favourably to Pharaoh's dreams.

Does Joseph have an opportunity to get bitter? Yes! The "butler gave no thought to Joseph, but forgot all about him." The Bible indicates that Joseph's soul was welded to the irons in prison. He had every opportunity to give up in despair while "he waited for the word of the Lord to be fulfilled."

Joseph's 'Fullness of Time'—The Pulpit

There is a God-appointed time for raising up an individual for great and powerful things. There is a "fullness of time" (Gal 4.4). If we maintain a humble and contrite heart, then "in due season He will raise us up" (1Pe 5.6). As we read through Genesis 41, the Bible says that "after two full years, Pharaoh dreamed." The dream had to do with seven fat and lean cows and seven ears of grain. Then the butler remembered Joseph.

Joseph was brought "hastily out of the dungeon. But first he shaved, changed his clothes, made himself presentable [note: what about us, before the King of Kings?], and came into Pharaoh's presence." One can only wonder at the many thoughts and feelings that were going through his mind. One can only surmise that Joseph sensed the divine timing involved. I can hear him speaking words of encouragement to himself, positioning his heart to be a voice of the Lord to a nation.

"How can I do this thing and sin against God?"

When Joseph opened his mouth, he stated, "God

Life Purpose

has shown Pharaoh what he is about to do [note: God's eternal purpose]." The interpretation of the dream became clear. The result? He was raised up to complete God's purpose for his own generation.

Joseph kept his integrity by serving authority faithfully: this made him the perfect individual to be placed in authority! If you cannot obey, you cannot command. He served the Lord's purpose by serving Potiphar and the warden. Now, he would serve the Lord's purpose by serving a secular king in a spiritual manner. He had kept his integrity by running from sin. He could have aborted God's life assignment and God would have had to raise up another. But Joseph believed his dreams were from God and His favour was more important to him than a moment of sinful pleasure.

Joseph kept his integrity by not abusing his position. This is demonstrated in three ways: first, his complete lack of revenge against Potiphar because of his wife; second, his lack of revenge against the butler; and, third, his lack of revenge against his brothers. He maintained his integrity throughout and the Lord raised him up. Joseph completed his life purpose in a glorious manner.

Joseph never gave up on the dream or its interpretation. He overcame the "trying of the Word of the Lord in him." It made him a man "thoroughly equipped for every good work" (Jas 1.4). Joseph recognized God's Hand upon his life and the part he had to play:

> Do not be distressed, or vexed and angry with yourselves because you sold me here, for God

had sent me ahead of you to preserve life—to preserve a posterity—so now it was not you who sent me here but God. You meant it for evil, but God meant it for good, to bring about that many people should be kept alive (Ge 45–50).

A Personal Testimony

Part of my personal life assignment is what I call *mission broking*, networking people to kingdom initiatives connected to bringing in this last days world harvest of souls. Early on, I came to understand that part of His calling on my life had to do with missions. I started praying for specific missionaries, expanded that to reading biographies and following mission reporting, and finally, to financing Kingdom initiatives.

I have been extremely privileged to be actively involved with developing mission initiatives in many nations over the last 30 years of ministry. There is not one nation that God has sent me to where He did not require me to sow financially towards that mission activity before I entered it. I am writing this part of the book from Oaxaca City, Mexico, and sitting with me in the hotel restaurant are the owners: a Mexican brother and sister who have a Kingdom business agenda.

My heart is to bring in the harvest, both at home and abroad. As a result of that God has directed me to be involved in numerous church plantings, developing

Life Purpose

relevant ministry training institutes for mobilizing and sending out disciples, strengthening and aiding organizations like YWAM, Wycliffe and World Serve, and helping to establish Kingdom business initiatives to finance world and local missions.

> **Joseph kept his integrity by not abusing his position.**

When you have been given a life assignment, it becomes abundantly clear what you are to say *"No!"* to and what you are to say *"Yes!"* to. Spiritual warfare becomes unclouded because the enemy always fights you in the realm of your assignment. Friendships become transparent because you are quickly able to recognize the people that God has sent into your life to accelerate completing the call as opposed to those who have another agenda to fulfill.

Let's get on with living this life to the fullest, the only way God intended His kids to live it: abundantly, accurately, and intentionally—becoming a living epistle that other generations can read to encourage themselves in living out their destiny.

> ***"One person with a commitment is worth more than 100 people who have only an interest."***
> Mary Crowley

David Kalamen

Chapter 15
A Word For All Seasons

Arthur Tennyson, brother of Alfred Tennyson, Poet Laureate, became blind as theresult of cataract. However, this did not sour his outlook. He remarked, "God has sent me to His night school."

Francis Gay, The Friendship Book (1985)

This is a true story.

Brenda was a young woman and someone invited her to go rock climbing, something she had never done before. Although she was very scared, she went with her group to a tremendous granite cliff.

While she was resting on a rock ledge, with hundreds of feet below her and hundreds of feet above her, the safety rope snapped against her eye and knocked out her contact lens. She looked and looked for it, but it just wasn't there.

Here she was, far from home, her sight now blurry. She became desperate and began to pray that the Lord would help her find it.

When she arrived at the top of the granite cliff, a friend examined her clothing for the lens, but found nothing. She sat down, despondent.

Life Purpose

She looked across range after range of mountains, thinking of the verse: "The eyes of the Lord run to and fro throughout the whole earth." She thought, "Lord, you see everything. You know exactly where my contact lens is. Please help me."

Finally, they reached the bottom and there was a new group of climbers going up. One of them yelled out, "Hey, anyone lost a contact lens?" An ant was moving slowly across the face of a rock, carrying it on its back.

Brenda's father is a cartoonist and he drew a picture of an ant lugging that contact lens with the words, "Lord, I don't know why You want me to carry this thing. It's awfully heavy. But if this is what You want me to do, I'll carry it for you."

Josh and Karen Zarandona

The last several years have been some of the most trying and difficult transition years of my life. I find myself right in the middle of a life purpose season I am not very comfortable with. Everything that was comfortable for me has been removed: nothing is as easy as it once was. The Lord has required of me things I have had difficulty giving. Where He has led me, I have not always wanted to go. There have been times of inner and outer rebellion. At times I have felt totally abandoned, broken, and confused.

> **At times I have felt abandoned, broken, and confused.**

The writer of Ecclesiastes, said to be the wisest man on the face of the earth, affirms two key truths that all of us can resonate with. Firstly, there are seasons to life. We can attest to this fact naturally and have also known it physically [for instance, 1-20, preparation years; 20-40, productive years; 40-60, provision years; and 60-80, protection years], and some of us have even discerned it spiritually. Secondly, there are multiple reasons for the season. That is where some of us short-circuit because the reasons are not that easily known and understood: at times there does not even appear to be any good reason for the season and we find it is difficult to carry on when it lasts and lasts and lasts.

The Profit of the Season

Look at the seasons by reading through Chapter 3 of Ecclesiastes, particularly verses 1-9. We ask what Solomon asked: "What profit was there to what I just went through?" We tend to be able to handle the travail and hard work if there is a profit in it: in financial benefit, in character development, in experience and training, and so on. Solomon states, "I have seen the travail which God has given to the sons of men to be exercised [trained] in it." Therefore, there is a training in the season we need.

Every season provides specific training that is needed for our personal development and future assignments. God is up to something big in our lives. He requires that we trust Him absolutely: the only

Life Purpose

way that we can really get the "peace that passes understanding" (Php 4.7) is to be in some situations that pass our understanding! How we handle ourselves in the midst of these seasons is critical to Kingdom advancement. Ecclesiastes 3.11 says, "He has made everything beautiful in His time." Every season He promises to make beautiful. Remember this song?

> **"Something beautiful, something good; all my confusion He understood. All I had to offer Him was brokenness and strife, but He made something beautiful of my life."**

If we are faithful to work and to do what is expected of us in the midst of the season, He will also be faithful to make something beautiful out of it. And, how many of you know, the beauty doesn't reveal itself in the beginning. The beauty in the season does not fully manifest until the season reaches its maturity. It is made beautiful "in His time," not our own, when we believe it should happen. So, "Let us not be weary in well doing, for in due season we shall reap, if we faint not" (Gal 6.9).

In your life there is a season for personal development and advancement. There is a time for emerging maturity. Your season has a clear beginning and a clear ending. You will know when it started and you will know when it is *completed*.

There is no way to plan for these seasons: Jesus said, "It is not for you to know the times or the seasons which the Father has put in His own power [authority]" (Ac 1.7). It is always hard for us to understand what God is preparing for those who love Him (1Co 2.9-10). The natural man can't figure it out; however, we can come to know the seasons by the Holy Spirit. The seasons and times of God in your life are discerned by the Spirit, not by the natural man. But God will reveal those things to us by His Spirit, in His time. Thank you, Lord!

> *Testing always precedes promotion.*

What in the World Are You Doing With Me?

There was a time when our seasons and times were in our own hands, under our own authority (Jn 7.6). But when we gave our life to God, He took charge of our personal development and maturity. He gave us the Holy Spirit so we could participate with Him in the seasons of our lives. Sometimes we act as unbelievers in the midst of the season and do our own thing, even resist it (for example, take a vacation from dealing with "stuff" in our lives).

Passing the Test in the Seasons of Our Life

The goal of every believer is to pass the test in

Life Purpose

its season; then we will know the reason. Testing always precedes promotion. Our life does not differ much from grade school. God will require that each of us prove our potential at one level before being promoted to another. When man attempts to elevate himself beyond his potential, failure is almost always inevitable. Self-promotion and any level of human promotion can never replace divine promotion. And divine promotion can only come through proving one's personal potential. Advancement is never based upon favouritism or prejudice. God watches how we handle ourselves in the seasons and the times of His working in our lives.

Just as a product is never used until it is tested and proven, a person is never used until he or she is tested and proven. In the tests, our personal potential will be proven. The tests come to prove our potential for greater opportunity. By the way, most opportunities are disguised as hard work, so few usually recognize them (Ann Landers). God is making you to match the mission that He has for you! Like Queen Esther, "Who knows if you have not come to the kingdom for such a time as this?" (Est 4.14).

Seasons and times of testing come to enable us to handle increase. Can you handle increase in your life? Increase will decrease if you do not make room for it: development will diminish unless you have the guts to face the changes—will you make room for it? It will mean going through a season of various trials in your life.

James 1.2-4 asserts that we are to welcome our

trials as a friend. When we do that, we can accept the proving of God and endure the adversity when we don't understand what's going on. It is because we know that He has our best interests in mind that we can believe He will make everything beautiful and complete in His time.

This will mean accepting greater responsibility for your life—can you handle it?

It will mean drawing up the courage to expand beyond your comfort zone. If you are not willing to dream bigger, your life will shrink: are you willing to believe that a greater thing, a greater work is being prepared just for you?

See your season as an opportunity to grow: *carpe diem*—seize it—treat it as a transition point between a good and a greater good. There are some things about you only time can prove! Potential cannot be unfolded without it. Trust His time.

It is not a question of God's love for you: it is a matter of competence! God permits the seasons of life to develop good character: "good character is the moral strength to maintain our pre-planned course of good intentions to fulfill God's will for our life regardless of opposition." We want to know God's will, but God wants you to know Him and the character and grace He has placed within you for the days ahead.

> **God is making you to match the mission that He has for you.**

A Personal Testimony

Those who are believers in God know that there is no testimony without a test. Ministers of the Gospel know there is no message without a mess. God specializes in teaching His leaders, His Word, by personal experience. Let me tell you about a few God-assigned seasons in my life.

One day in the early 1980s I felt led to go into the church office and spend some quality prayer time with the Lord, just waiting on Him to speak to me. I needed to know the *"next step."* I sensed I was to lay on my face before Him. Time passed very quickly. There were times of reading His Word, praying, sleeping, and meditating. It was a great time of communion, but my heart ached for a word on the "next step" for my life.

At the very end of my time with the Lord, I heard a very specific phrase enter my spirit and mind: "David, I want you to start preaching every message as if you had a chance to speak to the nation!" That word penetrated my heart and challenged me. I thought to myself, "What if the Canadian Broadcasting Company (CBC) called me tomorrow and gave me an hour to speak to my nation, what would I say?" I knew one thing: I would spend a very significant amount of time in prayer to get the Word of the Lord. God was saying to "start preparing every message like that, with that kind of passion and purpose."

That led me into a season of sobriety. The people around me began to see a difference in my speaking:

a new authority, a fresh anointing, a prophetic call, and into the mix, a word addressing the nation of Canada. There was a new intercessory release in my heart and a passion I had never known to see Canada experience a sea-to-sea encounter with God.

This freshness in the Lord directed me into a season of obscurity with my heart pounding to declare something to the nation, but limited to a local church congregation. When I asked the Lord why I was to prepare myself this way, without a venue for declaring this word to a nation, God firmly replied into my spirit, "Do not promote yourself or your ministry. My Son made Himself of no reputation. Only go where I put you in people's hearts."

This call and commission to prepare on a national level has never lifted from my heart. Slowly, within the next seven years, doors began to open to release the messages He had put in my heart, both locally and nationally. Sometimes God's assignments are sealed orders to be opened in His season, at the right time, with the right people, and in the right place. Still, we have to be faithful in the season of His calling, even if it is to a season of silent preparation. His day for your life will come. Don't throw away your confidence in Him.

Seasons of Darkness and the Apparent Contradiction of Faith

I believe it could be said of any true believer: their greatest desire is to see revival impact people, cities, and nations in an incredible transforming way. In our passionate pursuit of His presence, I have encountered what I call *"the contradiction of His visitation!"* We want God, His presence, and His will so very much, but then we struggle with what the "More, God!" actually means.

The simple truth is this: we are not able to sustain more of God without letting go of more of us. If He is to increase, we must be willing to decrease. That quite often directs good and godly people into seasons of darkness and times of apparent contradiction.

The signs of this struggle surround us. God's people are not very skillful at wisely handling conflicting signs of His purpose and presence: we enter a river of joy mixed with a river of tears; repentance mixed with an ugly exposure of the hidden motives of the heart; prosperity of spirit mixed with a poverty of soul; Kingdom advancement but also Kingdom conflict—"a new devil at every new level," just to name a few.

> *Do not promote yourself or your ministry.*

Seeing God's people move from compromise (in a culture that loves convenience) and endure substantial losses so that conviction can emerge requires a willingness to face the dark seasons of the soul. There will be times when we feel caught in a time warp, theologically, between the promises of God (which require a revelation and obedience) and the possession of those promises (which will require faith and endurance).

We can be comforted by the fact that these God-created wildernesses are simply cross over points between where we are now, and where God is taking us. Even "Jesus was led by the Holy Spirit into the wilderness to be tempted by the Devil" (Mt 4.1). The Lord wants our roots and foundations (our identity and being) firmly planted and established in Him. He is after the heart for "out of the heart flows all the issues of life" (Pr 4.23). The higher the building God is erecting, the deeper the foundation needs to be.

God isn't satisfied with us enjoying just the theological position of "Christ being in us" (Col 1.27), or of us being in Christ. He wants "Christ fully formed in us" (Gal 4.19). You and I both know there is a big difference between being born of the Spirit, being baptized in the Spirit, and continually being filled with the Spirit. There is so much more in God, and God wants to take us there. To reach that place we must understand His ways and not just His precepts.

Those Who Walk in Darkness

There lived a man many years ago who loved and feared the Lord and continually turned away from evil. God said, "There isn't a man like him on the face of the earth, a perfect and upright man" (Job 1.8). He was blessed on every level and the favour of the Lord was upon him. Even this man knew it: He wrote, "Oh that I were as in months past, as in the days when God preserved me; when His candle shined upon my head, and when by His light I walked through darkness" (Job 29.2-3, KJV). The friendship of God was over my tent (NAS).

Could a man who was so dearly loved and favoured by God also be the very same man who later desperately cried out, "So am I allotted months of vanity, and nights of trouble are appointed me. When I lie down I say, 'When shall I arise?' But the night continues, and I am continually tossing until dawn" (Job 7.3-4, NAS).

We do not know of any specific area in which Job sinned against God. Throughout the centuries many theologians have questioned whether or not this book should have even been in the Bible. What kept it there? The fact that Jesus spoke about Job and affirmed the book's credibility. But, Job has brought some of the real questions of life to the light: "How can God permit righteous people, who have been called out of darkness into the light, to go through seasons of darkness?"

The one thing we do know is this: Job saw something in the darkness, in the valley of the shadow of death, that he may not have been able to see anywhere else. At the end of the book we read: "I have heard of You by the hearing of the ear; but now my eyes see you" (Job 42.5, NAS). The word see is the word ra'ah in Hebrew which means "to experience!" Job experienced God in the dark in a way he had never experienced God before, and his latter days were blessed more than the beginning (verse 12).

> **"Lord, I don't want this to ever happen to me."**

When we read the book of Job, I think some of us have an unspoken request: *"Lord, I don't want this to ever happen to me!"* Our theology fits the pattern better if it happens to the ungodly or the unethical, but not to the righteous. However, Isaiah, the prophet, declared, "Who among you fears the Lord? Who obeys the voice of His Servant? Who walks in darkness and has no light?" (Isa 50.10, NKJV).

What we need to realize is that Ezekiel understood the meaning of that particular scripture. Carefully read through Ezekiel 14.23-24. The key verse is "and ye shall know that I have not done without cause all that I have done in it, saith the Lord GOD" (KJV).

In seasons of apparent contradiction, it is absolutely vital that we bring to remembrance Jeremiah 29.11, "For I know the thoughts that I think toward you, saith the LORD, thoughts of peace, and not of evil, to give you an expected end" (KJV). Romans 8.28 declares, "And we know that all things work together for good to them that love God, to them who are called according to His purpose" (KJV).

Oswald Chambers wrote, "the darkness . . . comes not on account of sin, but because the Spirit of God is leading us away from walking in the light of our consciences to walking in the light of His love" (*Biblical Psychology,* Oswald Chambers, page 180). Until we understand that these seasons have come from the Heart and planning of the Father, our lives will drift into utter confusion and reaction. He wants to teach us to see in the dark. He wants to bring our faith to the surface in the midst of the trial (Jas 1.1-5).

The Trying of Our Precious Faith

I don't know about you, but it always helps me when I am going through some incredible tests to know that other people have gone through similar challenges to their faith. When I read and ponder scripture, I know I am reading a book God would have written because of the integrity and transparency of the heart: "Man looks on the appearance but God looks on the heart" (1Sa 16.7).

Listen to some of the gloomy moments a few Bible greats expressed in their time of testing. Job uttered, "when I waited for light, there came darkness" (30.26). Jeremiah lamented, "my strength and my hope is perished from the Lord" (La 3.18). Jesus cried out, "Father, why have you forsaken Me?" (Mt 27.46).

We have all been there. We have felt the darkness, the sense of abandonment, the fear we had lost His love, the anxiety about trusting Him, the overwhelming disappointment, the desire to give up. What was God up to? Maybe analyzing this is not your thing, but it is mine. I need to know even the mysteries of God. I don't want to just go through something, but to come through understanding not only the acts of God but also His ways—the facts.

Many times in my life when darkness came and a sense of foreboding filled my soul, I came out fighting! For me there were only three biblical responses to such trials of my faith: repent, rejoice, or rise up and fight. I never knew anything about relenting and allowing God to be God in the situation, even if I did not understand it. No doubt you have heard the phrase *"let go and let God."*

Nothing reveals our true selves more than the incoming trials of life, going through the hard times. Sometimes it seems there is a light shining through the tunnel, but it is just another train coming through. Been there?

> **Repent, rejoice, or rise up and fight.**

In order to expose what is hidden way below the surface, mixed in with who we really are, God has to turn up the heat. Real high. It separates religiosity from relationship. It separates our confession (what we say with our mouth) from our faith (what we believe in our heart).

Life Purpose

All of us want to be able to see and understand what God is doing beforehand, so co-operation comes easy. We want to know why He is doing it and what He sees as the outcome. However, that is not faith. Real faith is not seeing, not understanding, not feeling, not knowing, but still trusting. Real faith believes God will perform His Word and His will in His way and in His time. Remember, we have an appointment with God, not a disappointment.

Faith is totally allowing God to be God in the midst of any apparent contradiction! God wants His faith formed in us, the kind of faith Christ had in His Father (Mk 11.22). He wants us to be like Jesus (Ro 8.29). When revelation successfully passes through this contradiction of the soul, we enter into a "peace which passes all understanding" (Php 4.7) and experience a "joy unspeakable and full of glory."

"In this you greatly rejoice, though now for a little while you may have had to suffer grief in all kinds of trials. These have come so that your faith—of greater worth than gold, which perishes even though refined by fire—may be proved genuine and may result in praise, glory, and honor when Jesus Christ is revealed. Though you have not seen Him, you love Him; and even though you do not see Him now, you believe in Him and are filled with an inexpressible and glorious joy, for you are receiving the goal of your faith, the salvation of your souls (1Pe 1.6-9, NIV)."

Night Seasons

Chuck Missler said that night seasons "are not ordinary trials, but specific transition times when God moves us away from depending upon 'self' to depending upon 'Him.' They are seasons when He strengthens our faith and teaches us to walk by the 'Spirit.'" Don't fret. The night seasons are God-sent.

Passing through these apparent contradictions of faith (enduring) is the only way true faith will emerge and for His will to be experienced (inheritance). Night seasons are the process God uses to replace us with Himself.

During the night season there is no apparent disobedience or sin. Heaven "seems" silent and a feeling of abandonment and disconnection from God's voice or His help pervades our very being. God deprives us of the "natural light" we have always depended upon to make our decisions (our own thoughts, feelings, ideas, and understanding), so that our faith is disconnected from the soul and brought into the spiritual dimension of our lives.

Don't fret!

The way of faith is not easy—it is a leap into the dark and a leap into the light at the same time. It will confound your logic, destroy all of your preconceptions, annihilate your religious attitudes, frustrate your goals, and probably alienate some of your friends. It's not the kind of faith the world

Life Purpose

teaches or even the church, at times, but it is the God kind of faith.

Andrew Murray related this. In time of trouble say, "First, He brought me here. It is by His will that I am in this strait place, in that I will rest." Next, "He will keep me here in His love, and give me grace in this trial to behave as His child." Then say, "He will make the trial a blessing, teaching me lessons He intends me to learn." And then say, "In His good time He can bring me out again. How and when He knows." Therefore, say, "I am here by God's appointment, in His keeping, under His training, for His time."

Illustrations for Biblical Preaching (page 388)

Chapter 16

Understanding the Mysteries of Life Through the Eye of Purpose

There is a story about a pregnant Rwandan mother of six whose village was destroyed by a massacre. She was shot and buried under the bodies of each of her six kids and left for dead. She dug herself out, buried her children, bore her new child, and thereafter chose to adopt five children whose parents had been killed in the same massacre. She expressed her belief that herlife had been spared so she might care for others.

Margaret S. Wheatley, *Turning to One Another* (page 59)

"The Lord GOD has given me the tongue of the learned, that I should know how to speak a word in season to him that is weary. He wakeneth morning by morning, He awakens My ear to hear as the learned. The Lord GOD has opened My ear; and I was not rebellious . . . For the Lord GOD will help Me; therefore shall I not be confounded: therefore I

Life Purpose

have set my face like a flint, and I know that I shall not be ashamed."

Isaiah 50.4-7, *New King James Version*

I am convinced that every life can be understood from the perspective of their individual life assignment. What appears as something mysterious becomes very clear when a person is able to see the events of their life through the eyes of God's eternal purpose! Unless we have that inner sense of mission, the circumstances of life have the potential to detour or derail us. We can wind up asking, as many people do, "Why do terrible things happen to good people?"

I am persuaded that God wants to establish His purpose so completely in our hearts that absolutely nothing can dissuade us from fulfilling His will. We can know His will, where we fit into His eternal purpose, and, like Christ, our eyes can be set like a flint on that which is set before us.

> **"Why do terrible things happen to good people?"**

Let me illustrate the above supposition with some Biblical illustrations. I am very aware there are things that happen in life that profoundly confound us, so I bring this to you as one who has been, and continues to be, a student of people's lives and an observer of scriptural patterns. I present this to you for your information, pleading that the Holy Spirit will make it a revelation to you.

King David

As you have been reading this book, you know his life well by now. But, for the purposes of this principle, let me reiterate.

David was a shepherd, chosen from among his brothers, and anointed to replace King Saul as the next king over Israel (1Sa 16.3, 13). The Lord said that he was a "man after My own heart, who will do all My will" (Ac 13.22).

As soon as David started acting on the anointing and this new commissioning, he experienced resistance and trouble—the giant Goliath (1Sa 17) and Saul (1Sa 18.7-9). So he escaped into the wilderness and dwelt in the caves, attracting a 3D company of men—men who were discontented, in distress, and in debt (1Sa 22.2).

This is where the story gets interesting. Even though Saul has as many as 3,000 men out looking for David, he escapes capture. Why isn't he captured? Because David knows he has been prophetically called to be the next king of Israel.

When David has an opportunity to kill Saul, his pursuer, and Abishai tells him, "God has delivered your enemy into your hands" (1Sa 26.8), he allows the opportunity to pass by. Why? Because David adamantly refuses to take destiny into his own hands but will leave the timing of entering into his life purpose, as king of Israel, in the hands of the Lord (verses 9-12).

Life Purpose

When David despairs of life and he goes into the land of the Philistines (1Sa 27.1), God raises him up to become the king's bodyguard (1Sa 28.2). He also receives protection from his enemies. They know him as the one who killed his ten thousands. Why isn't he killed? Because he kept his integrity (1Sa 29.5-9) and the prophetic word had not yet come to pass.

When David leaves his association with the Philistines, he inhabits a city called Ziklag. Read 1 Samuel 30. While out on a mission the city was raided by the Amalekites, burned with fire, and everyone in it was taken away—though they were not killed. When David's men found out what happened their hearts were broken and they even considered killing David, but he "encouraged himself in the Lord."

An interesting situation emerges. Even though David has lost his two wives, he seeks the counsel of the Lord and then asks a question that challenges us all: "Shall I pursue this band? Shall I overtake them?" What a question to ask! For many of us the question doesn't even merit being asked. It is more than self-explanatory. Should not a man go after his own family?

But David's heart is so yielded to God's will, in all things, that he will not do anything unless it is in absolute obedience to God's directive. What integrity in the midst of his worst nightmare! I can hear the voices all around him: "David must be out of God's will because of the evil that has fallen upon us!" I can hear the voices on the inside of him: "Why, God? Why would you permit this when I am trying to walk honorably before you in all that I do?"

> **Why God?**

That voice is quieted by the inner voice of the Spirit of God confirming to him that he is exactly where he is supposed to be, doing what he is supposed to be doing. All will be well. And, it was. He pursued his enemies and recovered all. When one sees the situation through the eyes of purpose, Ziklag was never intended to be David's city. God had other plans. God permitted this because He had a higher purpose in mind. Within months David was installed as king over Israel and Jerusalem would become known as the city of David. What a different chain of events would have occurred if David had not been willing to be obedient to the voice of the Lord.

Elijah the Tishbite

There are few Old Testament characters that inspire us as fully as Elijah. What a godly man! What amazing things were done through the fulfillment of his calling as a prophet to Israel. Few men have been given the level of anointing, combined with a level of testing that Elijah encountered.

Elijah means *"Jehovah is God!"* His background is sparse, but he appears to have been raised up by God to rid the land of its spiritual adultery and idolatry. He was living in a very polytheistic society. In time, Baal came to represent the idea of one god—all gods in one (the religious concept of pluralism); and

Life Purpose

therefore, competed with the belief in Yahweh, the One and only true God (Dt 6.4). Jesus alludes to this same spirit in His teaching and names him Baalzebub, meaning "lord of the flies," lord of the dwelling, prince of demons, a very specific reference to satan himself (Mk 3.22).

Elijah's primary competition was Jezebel, the wife of Israel's king, Ahab. She was a zealous Baal worshipper and tried to rid the nation of Israel of its godly priests and prophets (1Ki 18.4), supplanting their influence with Baal leadership: she had 450 of Baal's prophets eating at her table (1Ki 18.19). The spirit that was operating through her caused ten million Israelites to forsake their belief in God, other than the 7,000 faithful. She was as brazen as Elijah was bold. When Elijah boldly confronted her with sin and idolatry, she ruthlessly waged war against God's prophets and their righteousness. To the victor went the soul of a nation.

When Elijah decided it was time to meet King Ahab, he is seen as the "one who troubles Israel" (1Ki 18.17). During this dialogue Elijah proposes a test as to whether the Canaanite Baal or the Israelite God is the true God (1Ki 18.17-40). The God who answered by fire was the God to serve. To this more than challenging challenge, "the people answered him not a word," totally incriminating their double mindedness of heart!

Elijah knew a God of fire (1Ki 18; 2Ki 1). Six hours, then twelve hours passed concerning the test of fire. Then the fire of God fell. All of Baal's and Asherah's prophets were killed.

Everything Elijah did, he did by "the Word of the Lord." Read through 1Ki 17–18. He faced Ahab and Jezebel and the prophets of Baal and Asherah by the Word of the Lord. He shut up the rains of heaven and brought down the rains from heaven by the Word of the Lord. He got into trouble only when he failed to live by the Word of the Lord. When he hears of Jezebel's attempts on his life he runs, out of fear (1Ki 19), into the wilderness. There he wants to die. He is ministered to by an angel, twice. God takes him into a cave and asks him this question: *"What are you doing here, Elijah?"* God brings him to a mountain where the Lord passed by in a great wind, an earthquake, and a fire—teaching Elijah that He is in the still, small voice that can be heard in the spirit of a man. He is asked again: *"What are you doing here, Elijah?"*

> **To the victor went the soul of a nation.**

Why the repetition of questions? Because Elijah's destiny had been derailed by listening to the voice of a woman and not to the voice of God. Elijah was not where God wanted him to be. He was where he was through his own fears. He had gone from the mountain top of victory to the depths of despair in just a day, because he was no longer being led by the Word of the Lord. It resulted in what some people have thought to be an aborted mission: God orders a taxi from heaven, a chariot of fire to pick him up, and his life purpose is now concluded.

Life Purpose

Things happen in our life for a reason. Elijah's life purpose and assignment was cut short because he listened to the wrong word (and voice). Consequently, he was ordered to anoint Elisha to carry out his unfilled assignments. Elisha, through the pursuit of a double anointing, fulfilled Elijah's remaining assignments and his own as well.

Elijah's life and ministry must be seen through the eyes of the Lord's purpose. When a man or woman of similar passions and natural limitations as our own (Jas 5.17) draws back from destiny by carrying their own emotions and feelings to the point of outright resistance, it must be taken as a spiritual warning. All of us must place ourselves in a position of need to hear the Word of the Lord. Without the Word of the Lord, we are at peril and our destinies are at risk.

> *"Don't complain. The wheel that squeaks the loudest often gets replaced."*
> Anonymous

Chapter 17
Principles of Purpose

"It is better to die for something than to live for nothing."

Dr. Bob Jones, Sr.

"Adversity causes some men to break— others to break records."

William A. Ward

I am convinced that every person can know God' will for their life. However, in times of apparent confusion or contradiction, I have found "the principles of purpose" I have gleaned from my growing knowledge of God, His Word and character, have brought great comfort to my soul. Whenever the circumstances of life appeared to be running contrary to my understanding of His will, I have rehearsed these principles in my heart and they have become a wonderful source of strength and wisdom in my daily living.

When things happen that challenge your faith and appear to thwart His will being accomplished in your life, or cause you to question God's intent, it is a cardinal rule that you go back to the place where your foundations can be reviewed, restored, and strengthened. Allow the following principles of purpose to be established in your heart to such a degree that they become part of who you are, how you think, and therefore, how you behave.

> ***Principles of purpose produce purpose-driven people.***

God wants His people to be *"principle governed"* and *"Spirit led,"* rather than *"preference governed"* and *"sense led."* If we desire to be a purpose-driven people, it is essential that we have principles that guide our lives. Let me introduce to you what is becoming a growing list of principles that I live my life by. I am confident that you will establish your own unique set as your relationship with God grows.

These principles are not based upon a "positive" outlook on life: they have been built upon the substance of God's Word and the testimony of godly people. Our faith needs to have substance to it, and the Word of God provides that substance (Heb 11.1).

Principle #1

God's Purpose and Plans are Achievable

If there is anything that affirms to me the "achievability" of His purpose for my life, cities, and nations, it is the authority of His character and the evidence of prophecy. I have already addressed the matter of His character: if God said He would do it, He will do it; if God said He can do it, He can do it; if He said he would use a specific individual to bring it about, God is able to do it. Do you believe that?

The overwhelming testimony of scripture is this: when He commits to a plan and to using a person, He is committed to its success one-hundred percent.

Philippians 1.6 says—"For I am confident of this very thing, that He who began a good work in you will perfect it " (NASB). The Apostle Paul experienced this for himself. Many times he could have given up on the divine commissioning, or what he called the heavenly vision, but something sustained him. It was the confidence that the good work God began in him would be perfected through him, if he believed. The plan and purpose of God is achievable because the Lord is totally committed to bringing it to completion in our lives.

Psalm 138.8 says—that "The Lord will perfect that which concerns me . . . do not forsake the works of Your Hands." Are there things in your life that have not been "perfected" yet? Matters that have not come to pass, dreams that have not been fulfilled? God will perfect that which He has promised! The responsibility lies upon you to believe and God to perform!

Job 23.14 says—"For He performs what is appointed for me, and many such decrees are with Him"—there are many more plans He has in store for

Life Purpose

us. We are scheduled for an appointment with God, not a disappointment. That which He has promised will come to pass: conceive it, believe it, receive it, and walk in it. God is not only the Author of His purposes, but He is also the Finisher and Perfector of all that he has promised (Heb 12.2). That which God said was appointed for us, He said he would perfect and perform because "the steps of a righteous man are established by the Lord; and He delights in his way" (Ps 37.23). In spite of the odds we face in many situations, we must believe that what God says, stands. The testimony of numerous biblical characters should encourage us to believe for the completion of our race.

- Jesus completed His life purpose (Jn 17.4).
- Paul completed his race (2Ti 4.6-8).
- Joseph completed the word God assigned to him (Ge 37–50).
- Caleb completed it (Jos 14.1-20).
- Noah completed it (Ge 6–8).

> ***All of us desire to hear two words from our Heavenly Father.***

God's plans and purposes can not only be achieved, but also completed. If Jesus could fulfill the assignments the Father called Him to do and these other men of God could execute what God called them to do, is there any reason why we should not believe for the same?

All of us want to hear two words from our Heavenly Father: "This is My beloved Son in whom I am well pleased" (Mt 3.17) and, "Well done, thou good and faithful servant, enter in" (Mt 25.23).

If we are to enjoy a successful life, both of these factors are a definite requirement.

The Nation of Israel

What happened in the life of Israel should always be a source of encouragement to us as we pray for our own nations. If God could stick to His prophetic plan over the centuries, is it possible He will stick to His prophetic plan for our personal lives? If God has not given up on a people, will He give up on a person?

I have been reading Norma Parrish Archbold's book *The Mountains of Israel* as I prepare to travel to Israel with twenty of Canada's evangelical leaders in March of 2003. What an honour to be part of an historic Christian diplomatic mission that God has opened up to us. On account of this ministry opportunity, I have been studying Ezekiel 35–36: it is such a prophetic portion of scripture.

God covenants with His people, Israel, their own land (His land), unconditionally (Ge 28). If Israel sinned against this covenant, they would be scattered among the nations (Eze 36.19) and the land would become desolate. They did and they were (70 A.D. and 135 A.D.). For 2,000 years a key part of the Middle East was desolate and uninhabitable (Eze 6). Where great forests once stood, the hills were now barren.

Life Purpose

Note: Under Turkish control (1517–1917) people who owned property with trees on it were required to pay taxes; the trees were chopped down, allowing the land to become completely desolate.

In 1920 the League of Nations designated British-occupied Palestine as a homeland for the Jews; in 1948 Israel became a Jewish State; in 1967 after the Six-day war, Jewish people inhabited the heart of the land promised by God and they began returning home from all the nations of the world. God remembered His covenant with the people of Israel to bring them back into their own land, even while they were yet sinful (Eze 36.24-25).

From 1906–1990 over 250 million trees have been planted and the land has sprung to life: its trees are yielding its fruit, and its land is yielding its produce. God said that the land would shoot branches once again (Eze 36).

God knows how to bring a plan to pass, crossing every barrier of time, people, generations, and spiritual resistance. Israel stands as evidence to the achievability and perfection of purpose in the life of a nation. This brings hope to our heart.

> *If God has not given up on a people, will He give up on a person?*

Principle #2
Every Purpose Has Its Fullness of Time

Habakkuk wrote: "Record the vision and inscribe it upon tablets, that the one who reads it may run. For the vision is yet for the appointed time; it hastens towards the goal and it will not fail. Though it tarries, wait for it; because it will certainly come, it will not delay" (Hab 2.2-3, Open Bible). This is a habit that keeps the dream alive in our hearts. God's purposes are birthed at the exact moment and not a second early or late.

Paul reminds us there is an acceptable, good, and perfect component to the will of God (Ro 12.2). Some of our actions may be considered acceptable, even good, before God, though they may be actions made before or after their appointed time. In Matthew 21.28-31, Christ uses the illustration of a man who had two sons: one said he would not obey, but afterward did; the other said he would obey, but did not.

Loren Cunningham speaks of a common experience that every man or woman of God goes through as it relates to their fulfilling the will of God, a phrase he has coined *"the death of a vision!"* This principle affirms that everything God wants to do has to happen His way and our attempts at making it happen our way, in our own time, may interfere with His purposes. For example, Abraham's pursuit

Life Purpose

of a son his way—producing an Ishmael, versus a son God's way—producing an Isaac, or a son of promise.

There is a time for the Joseph's to emerge to direct nations, for the Moses' to rise up and lead an exodus, for the Joshua's to take cities, for the Nehemiah's to rise up and build cities, for the Elijah's to take on corrupt kings and queens, for the Esther's to respond to the call and become deliverers for a race: there is a time, a God-day, when that which is impossible is birthed and passes from a conception of the mind to a reality.

Principle #3
Every Purpose of God Has An Enemy

As one man so aptly said, there is *"no testimony without a test, and no message without a mess."* We have an enemy: his name is satan (1Pe 5.8-10). He is an adversary to everything God wants to do. Satan opposed the work of creation in the garden, will he not oppose those who desire to fulfill God's purposes in their generation?

Joseph didn't have an enemy until he communicated a dream: then he had to face his brothers. The shepherd boy, David, didn't have an enemy until he picked up the call of God to lead a nation: then he had to face a Goliath. Elijah didn't have an enemy until he opened up his mouth and declared the Word of the Lord to his nation: then he had to face a Jezebel. Paul didn't have an enemy until he responded to the heavenly vision: then he had to face some assassins.

This is a common test to all who are called. God reminds us that these are the same faith challenges that face all of God's people (1Pe 5.9). The enemy has to be resisted in faith and we are exhorted to run our race, persevering in joy (Heb 12.2).

The whole world, including the Church, is at war. We have an enemy, satan, who kills every prisoner he takes; however, we also have a Champion, Jesus, who came to set the captives free.

The war we are in is primarily fought with thoughts and words (2Co 10.3-5) and this results in real casualties—satan steals, kills, and destroys (Jn 10.10).

We know that the enemy resists God's people in the area of their possessions (Nu 13–14); nevertheless, when we hold fast to God's Word, we will bring forth a testimony with which we can overcome him again and again (Rev 12.7-11).

Never forget, we are fighting a spiritual battle—it requires spiritual weaponry (Eph 6.10-18); however, also remember that we fight from a place of victory that has been procured for us through our Saviour, Jesus Christ (Ro 8.31-39).

> *"There is no testimony without a test, and no message without a mess."*

Life Purpose

I have found the following to be true, and it has stabilized and encouraged me in the midst of the enemy's preoccupation with my downfall.

There is no testimony without a test—overcoming is based upon our testimony. A man or woman who wields the weapon of a testimony is very difficult to beat. The goal God has for us is to see us pass the test. In education, passing the test means moving up a grade, being promoted. In the school of hard knocks, passing means gaining a word of a testimony that enables us to overcome: it means being spiritually promoted.

Divine promotion and readiness for next steps comes from proving our faith (Jas 1.1-4) and character (1Pe 4.12-14). Divine promotion is not based upon race, color, gender, age, or experience, but upon His observation of how we fight the good fight of faith and keep our integrity through every test we encounter. What fiery-inferno will cause melt-down in your life? What frigid temperatures will cause you to freeze and become immobile?

God will not permit us to be tested or tempted above what we are able to bear (1Co 10.13). Tests come to prove to you what you have learned, not what you do not know. It would be rather foolhardy for a teacher to test Grade 6 students with Grade 12 material.

God wants us to pass. Passing reflects not only the student, but the Teacher as well: a good Teacher knows when to test His students, because passing or failing reflects the ability of the Teacher and the student. As in material products, nothing is ready for use until it is tested. We may not believe that we are ready, but our Teacher knows when we are—trust Him.

God desperately wants to see you promoted: your testing precedes promotion. Promotion to what? Larger assignments, broader responsibility, greater accountability, and with every new level of promotion—a new devil.

To be honest, pursuing God's purpose has opened my life up to much opposition. That opposition has come in many, many forms: personal—inner fears, insecurities, rebellion; peers—misunderstanding, rejection, slander; and, demonic—imagination, sickness, stress. However, called, anointed, and appointed people understand how to go and grow through these challenges and to see the challenge as a *proof of calling, or clear evidence* that they are on track.

The enemy's opposition to God's will functioning in your life can sometimes be a clue to, and an affirmation of, your calling. Sometimes you need to take your stand and announce to the enemy that you are pursuing your calling, no matter what, because demonic resistance only confirms the Word of the Lord. It has come to a point in my life that any lack of opposition makes me even more concerned as to whether or not I am on track.

I remember an incident that took place quite a number of years ago that will illustrate this principle. I had just been at the doctor's office, several weeks prior to a missions trip to Asia. He had spotted an unusual growth on my neck and had operated to investigate. What was supposed to be a few minutes and a few stitches became a lot more.

> **"I think we got it all!"**

The doctor's statement at the end of the operation was *"I think we got it all!"* My mind raced back to the threat of cancer I had faced years before. He sent it away for a biopsy and asked that I cancel any trips I may be planning. I came home just a little distressed by the news and needing a little tender loving care from my family.

My daughter, Kerri, was the first to meet me and she inquired how things were. I asked for a hug: she gave me a hug and a long lecture. Her first question was *"Has the Lord requested that you go to Asia? Has He confirmed that to you?"* My answer was very clear: "Yes, honey, He has!" She looked at me and replied, "Well, you are going to be all right then. The biopsy will be negative." It was. I went and fulfilled God's assignment with an unusual level of anointing and access to people in all levels of authority.

Principle #4
All Things Work Together for Good

When we are on assignment from heaven, with

sealed orders to deliver His Word to a people, we can have full confidence that the undertaking shall be fulfilled. A few years ago I was dropped off at the Chiang Kai-shek Airport terminal in Taipei, Taiwan. I had attempted to check in for a midnight flight to Tainan for a ministry time the next day; however, my Canadian Airline ticket had been rejected and my rides had left.

I can still remember the tremendous sense of loneliness I felt standing there at the desk, on a holiday week-end, trying to find a way to my destination. But, I will also never forget the peace that came over me as I set to pray about the situation and how the Lord wrote Romans 8.28 upon my heart. He led me to approach the counter again and request a seat on another flight. They had one, and I boarded the plane with gratitude.

As I took my seat next to a well-dressed Taiwanese man, I heard these words come tumbling out of my mouth: *"You look like a general!"* He looked at me and said, *"Who told you I was a general?"* In a moment of time I knew why the Lord had altered plans and planes: He had another assignment for me. My statement had his attention. I said: *"God told me!"* and I began to share with him the entire message of Christ. He was a secular Buddhist, but one whose soul was apprehended by God. As a footnote to that. Almost ten years later a missionary we have in the region was asked to be involved with a Taiwanese man, teaching him English. Guess who the man was? You got it!

> "Who told you I was a general?"

The Apostle Paul

You will recall the dramatic conversion of Saul (Apostle Paul) in Acts 9. In that account is a description of Paul's "heavenly vision," which he clarifies as the substance of his calling or life purpose. One of the Apostle Paul's multiple assignments was that he "be a chosen instrument, bearing His Name before the Gentiles and kings."

During Paul's ministry, as reported in the book of the Acts of the Apostles, he is repeatedly told that if he travels to the city of Jerusalem, he would be taken prisoner and sent to Rome to stand before Caesar. In one specific situation, a respected prophet, Agabus, prophesied to him: "He took Paul's girdle, and bound his own hands and feet, and said, 'Thus saith the Holy Ghost, So shall the Jews at Jerusalem bind the man that owneth this girdle, and shall deliver him into the hands of the Gentiles'" (Ac 21.11, KJV).

They all cautioned him not to go to Jerusalem. But Paul answered, "What mean ye to weep and to break mine heart? for I am ready not to be bound only, but also to die at Jerusalem for the name of the Lord Jesus. And when he would not be persuaded, we ceased, saying, 'The will of the Lord be done'" (Ac 21.13-14, KJV). Paul knew something they did not understand concerning his God-ordained life assignment.

When Paul went to Jerusalem, he was caught and bound (Ac 22-23). Because of his Roman citizenship, he is put on a ship and sent to Rome to stand before Caesar. Scripture records that a contrary wind and no small storm arose that threatened the ship and the crew's lives (Ac 27.10). Paul then receives an angelic visitation. I personally believe that these divine visitations accompany people as a confirming force in the most difficult situations.

Paul announced this to his shipmates in Acts 27:

> "And now I exhort you to be of good cheer: for there shall be no loss of any man's life among you, but of the ship. For there stood by me this night the angel of God, whose I am, and whom I serve, saying, Fear not, Paul; thou must be brought before Caesar: and, lo, God hath given thee all them that sail with thee. Wherefore, sirs, be of good cheer: for I believe God, that it shall be even as it was told me. Howbeit we must be cast upon a certain island (22-26, KJV)."

Why doesn't Paul die in some Mediterranean mishap? His assignment was still activated! When the ship's occupants land on the island of Malta (Ac 28.1), they gather sticks to create a fire to warm themselves. Paul accidentally gathers up a poisonous viper that bites him. The locals believed he was an evil man and would die. Paul did not die. Why not? The mission had not been accomplished yet—he had not testified before Caesar. Paul then led the island into a revival through healing the sick, and then, going on to Rome to give a defense for his faith.

I sincerely believe that when we are on assignment and our lives are being lived out uncompromisingly, then we can enjoy a greater degree of confidence and boldness in living out our life purpose. I believe that when we encounter great difficulties like the Apostle Paul, we need to comprehend that we are in the situation because of obedience to His purpose for our lives and not by our own choosing. It is our only hope and confidence of all things working together for our good!

Nigeria

Let me illustrate! For a number of weeks I had been in early morning prayer with some of my staff. During this time the Lord kept bringing to my spiritual eyes a mass of black faces. It led me into a season of fervent prayer and intercession for my brothers and sisters in Africa. Then one day a fellow evangelist spoke with me, and he invited me to go to Nigeria with him in a ministry outreach.

My immediate answer was *"no!"* when he reminded me that I had to take a cholera shot. I had experienced a severe reaction to a previous cholera vaccine shot years earlier, prior to a ministry trip to Sri Lanka. I had almost lost my life and have thirty-six hours missing in my memory.

I requested him to ask my associate if he sensed a

leading to go to Nigeria. When my associate returned, saying, *"David, I really believe that God is asking you to go!"* I realized that my fears, rather than faith, were dictating my response. Right away I went to the Lord in prayer and to my wife for a confirming word. Prayer had been validating this invitation and my wife found an incredible peace about my going (I think she may have added, "Make sure that your life insurance is paid up!"). Anyway, I felt that taking another cholera vaccination would be the test the Lord would have to bring me through.

> **I like to refer to it as the "woman of my dreams."**

The night before the vaccination, I had a dream. I like to refer to it as the *"woman of my dreams."* She was a nurse at the clinic. She said to me, *"Come on in! Jump up on the bed! Stick your right arm out!"* I remembered the dream. Again, may I add that this kind of God-dream does not come unless you are already moving towards the goal of the upward call.

When I arrived at the clinic the next day, I was required to sign a form that released the medical staff from any future claim I may have against them for giving me the cholera shot. A voice called me into the nurses' station. When I got into the room I met the woman of my dream who said, *"Come on in! Jump up on the bed! Stick your right arm out!"*

That was not the way it had been done before whenever I had ventured overseas on a missions trip.

Life Purpose

The nurse had always stabilized my arm on a pull-out from the desk and put the injection into my left arm. However, when she said what she did, the peace of God hit my heart. The Lord had confirmed my going to Nigeria in a very supernatural way. There was no reaction, and today the world is my mission field by His grace and call.

I might also add that Nigeria was in a very difficult state at the time of my visit. Pastors were being killed and churches set ablaze. I had six weeks of ministry opportunities in extreme adversarial conditions, often ministering to 20,000 plus people at a time; a sea of black faces, the faces that were in my heart in prayer back home in Canada.

The last ministry night before my departure from Nigeria, the Lord directed me to take nothing but my Bible. He also instructed me to share my testimony of healing and to preach on healing. The meetings lasted well into the early morning hours as the neighbourhood continued to bring the sick to be prayed for, and then they listened to their testimonies of miraculous healings.

That extended period of time in ministry put me well beyond curfew. This was Lagos, not your average North American suburb. Heading home we were stopped by several machine gun wielding Muslim soldiers. When they saw an *'American'* in the vehicle, they immediately ordered I give them everything I had on me. When they opened the trunk, they saw no luggage. I had no identification, no money, or wallet. I offered them my Bible. In frustration, they angrily permitted us to travel on.

What kept me alive? It was the confidence I had that I was on a divine assignment, and I had obeyed the word of the Lord! The spirit of fear could not prevail against the Spirit of faith. God had prepared me for ministering in the miraculous power of healing by bringing me through my own test of trusting Him. The enemy's attack on my physical body had become a confirmation of empowerment for ministry.

Principle #5
Rejecting the Call May Mean Being Replaced

As I have repeatedly stated, the important thing is what God is doing, not what we are doing. Even though we may fail in our obedience and be faithless, God remains faithful to do what He has promised. The Bible says He cannot deny His own nature and character: "If we believe not, yet He abideth faithful: for [God] cannot deny Himself" (2Ti 2.13, KJV).

God doesn't change His mind when we change ours. God doesn't shift His plans when we change our plans. His purpose will stand. Though God invites, calls, and chooses to use man to fulfill His eternal purpose, our stubbornness to the call does not sabotage His intentions. He has the power to promote one and demote another: Psalm 75.6-7 says, "Promotion cometh neither from the east, nor from the west, nor from the south. But God is the judge: He puts down one, and sets up another" (KJV). His will shall come to pass.

> **The important thing is what God is doing, not what we are doing.**

It is important to remember this truth: God has an eternal purpose; that purpose will come to pass; He has invited us to partner with Him in promoting His purpose in this present generation; and that summons is an incredible privilege. Paul understood this and conveyed the following personal concerns to the church at Corinth.

> "Do you not know that in a race all the runners run, but only one gets the prize? Run in such a way as to get the prize. Everyone who competes in the games goes into strict training. They do it to get a crown that will not last; but we do it to get a crown that will last forever. Therefore I do not run like a man running aimlessly; I do not fight like a man beating the air. No, I beat my body and make it my slave so that after I have preached to others, I will not be disqualified for the prize (1Co 9.24-27, NIV)."

We see this principle of replacement in people and in nations. Let's look at some illustrations of both.

People

When Moses did not honor the Lord before the people, but spoke out of his own frustration, he was replaced by Joshua and was not given the opportunity to bring Israel into their promised land (Nu 20.10-12).

When Elijah became more caught up with creating a reason for not doing what the Lord had told him to do, God sent a taxi from heaven to pick him up and gave the assignment to another who would "take his place"—Elisha (1Ki 19).

When Saul's disobedience turned to rebellion, attempting to please man and gain the strength of man rather than God, God raised up another man whose heart was fully committed after Him, to fulfill His purpose for a nation (1Sa 13.13-14).

When God granted Peter an opportunity to open the doors to the Gentiles through various visions of His grace, Peter stood with his Jewish tradition rather than the revelation of God. He was removed from his place of leadership among the apostles and replaced with James (Ac 10; 21.18).

Nations

When Israel rejected God's intention expressed through the covenant God made with Abraham (Ge 12.1-3), God raised up another Man (Christ) and another nation (the Church) who would bring the

Life Purpose

blessing of the knowledge of the Lord to the nations (Jn 10.16; Ro 11.11-21). There is no nation on the face of the earth, whether or not they sense a manifest destiny, who can take fulfilling His purposes lightly. To sin against God's purpose for a nation's existence, or to distort His image of what a nation was raised up to be, is to sin against that nation's future. It may result in a nation losing its way, so to speak, and being replaced by another nation as the primary influence of righteousness, until it is reconciled to God. Then, and only then, will the nation come back and be ingrafted into a place of divine usefulness (Ro 11.24).

> **An unrepentant nation will be replaced by nations who will obey God's laws.**

Great Britain/United States—space is too limited for me to give you an in-depth study into the nation of Great Britain, its connection to the United States, and the state they both find themselves in today. It is amazing to see how a nation's world influence can diminish so rapidly whenever it fails to uphold righteousness, or fails to use its resources to expand godly kingdom influence. At this point in time it is only a national awakening (a reconciliation to God's original intent for a nation's birth) that can bring either nation back to a place of divine influence and once again stir up their destiny. Otherwise, an unrepentant nation will be replaced by nations who will obey God's law.

Let's wrap this up in a statement that wraps it up. Frank Damazio penned:

> "It is God who is in charge of every nation and people. When any nation [or people, person] breaks the laws and principles of God, sooner or later He will judge that nation. Security cannot continue in the presence of sin *(God's People Triumphant in Perilous Times, page 144)*."

> **"People and countries search for their identity only when they have lost their place of calling."**
> Paul Marshall

Life Purpose

Chapter 18
Delightful Daily Disciplines

"We are blind until we seeThat in the human planNothing is worth the makingIf it does not make the man.Why build these cities gloriousIf man unbuilded goes?In vain we build the worldUnless the builder also grows."

Edwin Markham

Healthy things grow. Growing things change. Changing things challenge.

Anonymous

When God calls a man or woman to be part of His army, He subjects them to the same rigorous training that all military personnel undergo in the natural: boot camp. It is here that every enlisted person must apply themselves for the work of their calling. It is time spent in boot camp that reveals whether or not a soldier is willing to pay the price to be used for active duty.

Without these daily disciplines we are at the mercy of other voices, feelings and circumstances, and directives. If we have not honed these skills, when God does speak to us about life purpose and where it fits into His ultimate plan, then we will not be disciplined sufficiently to hear, heed, and persevere. Is is worth it?

2 Timothy 2.3 says, "You therefore must endure hardship as a good soldier of Jesus Christ." Still want to enlist?

> *It is time spent in boot camp that reveals whether or not a soldier is willing to pay the price to be used for active duty.*

Discipline #1
Be God-Conscious

The first discipline is developing the ability to hear the *"still, small voice"* of the Lord (1Ki 19.12). You must be focused on what God is saying and doing! When your life is God-centered, you will find yourself available for spiritual service and divine appointment! God is not going to employ the sluggard, disinterested, or unavailable. He is looking for those who are prepared for assignments of divine importance.

Too often God's saints are not God-focused. Instead, they are, or have become self-conscious and internally driven (2Ti 3.2). They give God little attention and when they do talk to Him, they seldom leave room to listen. No wonder their lives are "forms of godliness without power" (verse 5).

Life Purpose

They can become world-conscious and others-centered (1Th 2.1-6). When we permit what other people say and expect to rule who we are and what our life is to be, we frustrate God's grace and calling. King Saul's reign was cut short because he feared the people. Many great men and women have had to go it alone (for example, Daniel), fight against the tide of public opinion (Noah), and decide to depend solely upon God (Sarah). 1 John 2.15-17 is key here: "Do not love the world or anything in the world. If anyone loves the world, the love of the Father is not in him" (NIV). Demas had a love affair with the world system and lost his life purpose (2Ti 4.10).

Many become circumstance-driven and feeling-centered (Jonah). Too often God's people permit circumstances to rule their thinking. Instead of becoming principle-based character people, they are like spiritual chameleons, changing with every wind of influence: their feelings rule rather than God's Word.

Unfortunately, this generation is living in the midst of many voices and is finding it difficult to hear the Father's voice clearly for themselves. This discipline must be cultivated and nurtured through increased time in prayer and reading the Word of God. If not, confusion will dominate the emotions, leading to a shipwrecked faith (1Ti 1.18-19).

The sin many of us fall into is not that we shake our fists at God and defy Him to His face—that is the sin of those who don't know God: the unbeliever. The common sin of the Church is that we passively rebel against God, filling our lives with so much noise and busyness that God's voice is just one of many and quite difficult to discern (Gary Thomas, *Seeking the Face of God,* page 98).

One of the ancients wrote:

> "God does not cease speaking, but the noise of the creatures without, and of our passions within, deafens us, and stops our hearing. We must silence every creature, we must silence ourselves, to hear in the deep hush of the whole soul, the voice of our Spouse. We must bend the ear, because it is a delicate and gentle voice, only heard by those who can no longer hear anything else (Fenelon, Christian Perfection, pages 155-156)."

Cultivating a quiet time with God—more listening than our talking—is a very difficult thing when this generation has become so addicted to noise, excitement, and entertainment. Opening the door to spiritual quiet can also open the door to our greatest fears: it takes courage to come before God alone. It takes courage to confront ourselves, to see what God sees and not to try and cover our pain with a party.

It takes courage to confront ourselves, to see what God sees and not to try and cover our pain with a party.

Life Purpose

Pascal, in his book Pensees (page 38), believed that many people live a fundamentally dishonest existence, pretending they are having a good time when they live in constant terror of the truth of their hearts. Their lives are all noise, diversions, and thoughts for the future. But take away their diversion and you will see them bored to extinction.

Augustine saw this predisposition, in youth, as the drive to play; in adults, the drive for busyness and business. Quoting Pascal once again, he wrote: "The thing we fear most is quiet. Our lust for diversion proves our unhappiness, for if we were truly happy we would not need to divert ourselves from thinking about it." The chaos of the soul, the busyness of the spirit, both rob us from our created destiny. A voice within tells us that something is wrong, but we are much too afraid to slow down and find out how different life could be.

Gary Thomas stated that trying to change after years of being addicted to the narcotics of noise will not happen easily. We cannot have a life filled with diversions one day and the next day walk hand in hand with God, communing with Him, without paying the price of withdrawal. Our souls will roar for diversion, the "fix that saves us from God's presence" *(Seeking the Face of God,* page 101).

It is important to cultivate the discipline of letting go of any information that does not concern us. Listening to His voice and what He wants us to do so that we can intelligently say "No!" to other matters that would take us away from our life purpose is key. We can do all things through Christ's empowerment, but we are not being called by Him to do all things (Php 4.13). There is one thing we must do, and do well (Php 3.12-14).

These are perilous days we are living in, the last of the last days! It will be critical that each believer know the voice of God, and after hearing it, obey. There has never been a greater requirement for the prophetic voice declaring the will of God to a generation! However, when a people no longer have prophetic ears to hear prophetic truth and direction, the Church [and the world] is in trouble, deep trouble.

One of the key words in the book of Jeremiah is the word to *"listen."* The meaning in Hebrew is "to perceive a message, to give attention, to hear effectively and critically, to hear with understanding so as to result in obedience." The Greek word *akoue* referred to as hearing in Romans 10:17 simply implies this: if you have heard and have not done, you have not heard.

Hearing God requires more than showing up in Church, reading a passage of scripture before you go to bed at night, or reading from the promise box: hearing is understanding, and understanding requires obedience—reshaping your entire life to align itself with Biblical and prophetic truth. Only when a word is allowed to shape us can we say that we have really heard. The Taylor translation of 2 Timothy 3.5 states, "they will go to Church, yes, but they will refuse to allow what the preacher is preaching to change them!"

There are three ways we can cultivate a discipline of God-consciousness: meditate on His Word; pray; and praise.

> **The Greek word *akoue* simply implies this: if you have heard and not done, you have not heard.**

Meditate On His Word

Why is it beneficial for you to study and meditate on scripture? Because God has established His Word as a primary tool in leading and guiding our life! A lack of studying His Word will leave us desolate and unprepared for an assignment. Jesus told us that "man cannot live on bread alone, but needs every word that God speaks" (Mt 4.4, GNB).

Jesus said that His disciples had to be disciplined ones in the Word: if they disciplined themselves accordingly, they would know the truth and the truth would set them free (Jn 8.31-32). Without knowing the written Word, we will have a difficult time hearing the living Word. We will be left to locate our own manual for life and wind up dangerously building our future on a sandy foundation (Mt 7.24-27).

We must get our priorities in order for His Word to have a supernatural affect. The Word of the Lord must mean more to us than materialism because "cares of the world, delight in riches, the desire for other things" choke the effectiveness of God's Word (Mk 4.18-19). Time spent with Him must be more important than our activity apart from Him. John of the Cross wrote in his book *The Ascent of Mount*

Carmel that "the more people rejoice over something outside of God, the less intense will be their joy in God." What God has to say must mean more to us than our own or our culture's humanistic ideas (Ro 1.21). Application must be more important than information gathering.

Reading, hearing, and heeding God's Word not only tells us about Christ, but it actually brings Christ to us. Examining the scriptures ensures that our faith is firmly rooted, like the Bereans (Ac 17.10-11). Colossians 3.16 states, "Let the Word of God dwell richly in you as you teach, admonish and train one another in all insight, intelligence, and wisdom."

Proverbs tells us that we need to dig for this wisdom as we would lost treasure (Pr 2). King David said, "How shall a young man cleanse His way? By taking heed and keeping watch [on himself] according to Your Word [conforming his life to it]. Your Word have I laid up in my heart, that I might not sin against You" (Ps 119.9-11). When you meditate on God's Word, it will become a lamp to your feet and a light unto your path (Ps 119.105). So, if you truly desire your life to have a favourable outcome, be like Joshua who listened to and meditated on the Word of God day and night (Jos 1.8). Then apply it to your life.

Each and every one of us must choose! The mind of man or the mind of the Lord? The voice of confusion or the voice of reason? The opinions of a worldly system or aged truth that liberates? You must choose if you want to have the theories of man operating in your life or the principles of God!

Whatever dominates your thinking will dominate your future. Proverbs 23.7: "As a man thinks in his heart, so is he!" I believe that my destiny is linked to what I feed my mind! "Set your mind on things above" (Php 4.8) because right thinking will produce right living!

Pray

Prayer affirms to God that His perspective concerning your life matters! Climacus, author of the book *The Ladder of Divine Ascent,* said: "Intelligent silence is the mother of prayer, freedom from bondage, custodian of zeal, a guard of our thoughts!"(page 158). He felt that those who talked the most, prayed the least. The true mark of a spiritual man or woman is surely a listening heart, not a lecturing tongue.

God has always desired to speak to His people! Read through Genesis 3 and you will find it was not a lack of God speaking, but of man listening!

> *My equation for prayer is this: ninety percent listening plus ten percent talking.*

It is surely a lack of our listening that gets us into trouble. Much of the confusion that we experience in terms of knowing the will of God has not as much to do with God talking as with our insensitive, and possibly selective, hearing. Christians should not lead boring lives. If we are, it is not so much God not speaking to us as it is a lack of radical obedience to do what He requires!

All throughout scripture, the paths of God's men and women have been Spirit-led. Many of them did not have the Word of God as we do today! However, even when they did, many of them received things from God that no written word from God could ever affirm to them as being from God: for example, Noah building an ark; Abraham leaving his home and looking for a city whose Maker and Builder was God; Peter walking on the water, and so on.

These men and women simply had to know God, listen to His voice, and obey! The only way that can happen is by their developing a consistent prayer life. My equation for prayer is this: it is ninety percent listening plus ten percent talking.

The more time you spend with God, the more familiar you will become with His voice. The Apostle James even comments on the powerful prayers of Elijah (5.16-18). God hears the prayers of righteous men and women because righteous prayers have power. But Elijah was also afflicted in the area of his emotions, just as we are. When he failed to pray and listen to God he got himself into some real trouble; however, when he heard God's voice within—"the breath of a light whisper" (1Ki 19.12, Mof), he prevailed!

If Jesus spent a significant amount of time in prayer, what about us? Prayer is a required discipline in graduating from boot camp. It is the very thing that delights the heart of God. Prayer must be a

Life Purpose

priority and a lifestyle. It will ensure that each one of us knows the plans and purposes of God without a shadow of a doubt.

Two ingredients for a successful prayer life are a certain *time* and a certain *place*. Why is this so important? Because prayer is a flow and a rhythm! Prayer is not something you do, it is something you are; you are a pray-er!

Jesus did not get caught up in crisis prayer events: He went from prayer event to prayer event, and in between, took care of every crisis. His life was a lifestyle of prayer: Jesus preached, prophesied, taught, cast out devils, and healed the sick in between critical points of prayer. He developed His prayer life.

Prayer is not something that can be taught: it is something that is caught. You catch the spirit of prayer by being in prayer, by praying alongside prayer warriors. *"If you give Me the first hour of the day, I will change your life!"* Maybe you don't believe that even God gets up at that hour. Prayer is the highest calling in our life. Christ's testimony is that something supernatural happened every day as a result of His commitment to pray! It can't be comprehended any other way than as a result of prayer. It is a master key to an overcoming life.

> ***Who will you worship?***

David Kalamen

Praise and Worship
Sing to the Lord "A New Song."

Read and meditate on Psalm 149. You will soon understand why praise and worship is one of the most critical disciplines of the purpose-led life.

We were created to worship God (Rev 5.13); therefore, it is a natural thing. When man sinned in the Garden and fell away from God, his heart turned from worshiping God to creating gods he could worship (Ro 1.21-25). When this confusion over who was to be worshiped occurred, man lost his sense of direction and destiny and confusion entered his heart (Ro 1.28-32).

The battle since Creation is over the issue of worship: *"Who will you worship?"* Who is worthy of your attention? Even Christ faced this. His victory over satan established Him in His own identity as the Son of God and also maintained His connection to His Father's will and purpose (Mt 4.9-10).

In the Old Testament, after the Fall of humanity, God set up a sacrifice for sin. Each one brought their very best to Him. It was a sacrifice! When Christ died for us His blood was the ultimate sacrifice, abolishing the blood sacrifices that had been in place; however, sacrifices were not cancelled altogether. One sacrifice was still required: the writer to the Hebrews referred to it as *"the sacrifice of praise"* (13.15).

God seeks the fellowship of those who will worship Him in Spirit and in truth (Jn 4.23-24). Scripture affirms that God inhabits the praises of His people (Ps 22.3). God is attracted to the worshipper. Praise is becoming and appropriate to a child of God (Ps 147.1). Praise is an act of the will that encourages the mind to think about God (Col 3.16) and the emotions to feel after Him (Ac 17.27-28).

Praise and worship discloses how much God means to us: it is not centered on our sense of worthiness to praise Him as much as it is on His worthiness to receive it (Rev 4.11). When we give Him the sacrifice of praise, closed doors open: Paul and Silas (Acts 16,); walls that have interfered with our forward advancement into His purposes, come down: Jericho (Jos 6); we are released out of our captivity to circumstances and put back on track: Jonah.

God is not looking for "auto-pilot" praise! The will must be engaged, the mind directed towards the Lord, the emotions released as an expression of the heart (Ps 103.1-3). This act, this spiritual habit, this godly lifestyle is an essential key to the ongoing discovery of your life purpose.

So start off your day the right way. Sing unto the Lord a new song!

Discipline #2

Wear a Cloak of Humility

The disciple cannot be greater than His Teacher. It is well enough that he be like His Teacher: "The disciple is not above his master, nor the servant above his lord" (Mt 10.24). If we want God to consistently employ us, we have no choice but to clothe ourselves with the humility of Jesus Christ. "Let Christ be your example as to what your attitude [in life] ought to be—He humbled Himself" (Php 2.5-8).

James writes this: "Humble yourselves—feeling very insignificant—in the presence of the Lord, and He will exalt you—He will lift you up and make your lives significant" (4.9-10, AMP). Peter, who himself suffered humiliation because he betrayed Christ, conveyed this thought for the benefit of all Christians:

> "God sets Himself against the proud—the insolent, the overbearing, the disdainful, the presumptuous, the boastful, and opposes, frustrates and defeats them—but gives grace (favour, blessing) to the humble. Therefore humble yourselves (demote, lower yourselves in your own estimation) under the mighty hand of God, that in due time He may exalt you (1Pe 5.5a-6; Pr 3.34, AMP)."

Humility is a mystery to many.

Humility is critical to successfully completing our journey with God. We are on the road to success when we walk with bowed heads and knees, recognizing Who walked before us and the incredible price He paid for our spiritual freedom.

Humility is a mystery to many in this generation: its *modus operandi* is more characterized by advancing

Life Purpose

self and private agendas, no matter the cost. Modern man confuses humility with humiliation. We are more likely to see false humility, the result of superficial living, than we are to see "lowliness of mind" Greek tapeinophrsume (Php 2.3). Nelson's Illustrated Bible Dictionary defines biblical humility as "a freedom from arrogance that grows out of the recognition that all we have and are comes from God." The Greek philosophers despised humility because it implied inadequacy, lack of dignity, and worthlessness. Biblical humility is not belittling self (Ro 12.3), but an exalting or praising of others, especially God and Christ (Jn 3.30; Php 2.3). A humble person, then, focuses more on God and others than on himself.

Biblical humility is also "a recognition that by ourselves we are inadequate, without dignity, and worthless." Yet, because we are created in God's image and because believers are in Christ, we have infinite worth and dignity (2Co 4.6-7). True humility does not produce pride but gratitude. Since God is both Creator and Redeemer, our existence and righteousness depend on Him (Jn 15.5).

For the Christian, *the way up is down*. God's people must walk the road least travelled and go down into the valley of humiliation before reaching the mountain top of victory. It is the way of the cross. Until we really understand dying to self, we will never experience the resurrection life of God. Paul said it well: *"We must share His suffering if we are to share His glory"* (Ro 8.17).

The way down is the way of the cross. Paul wrote of a very different crowd in the Church:

> "There are many out there who are taking other paths, choosing other goals, and trying to get you to go along with them. I've warned you of them many times; sadly, I'm having to do it again. All they want is easy street. They hate Christ's cross. But easy street is a dead-end street. Those who live there make their bellies their gods; belches are their praise; all they can think of is their appetites. But there's far more to life for us (Php 3.16-19, TMT)."

The Tay translation says they are "proud of what they should be ashamed of" (verse 19).

A crossless Christianity results in a counterfeit, superficial, pseudo-Christianity. Paul warned the Church to "keep a sharp eye out for those who take bits and pieces of the teaching that you learned and then use them to make trouble. Give these people a wide berth. They have no intention living for our Master Christ. They're only in this for what they can get out of it" (Ro 16.18, TMT).

For the Christian, the way up is down.

Look at what transpired in Christ's life when He yielded Himself to the way of the cross. When He humbled Himself, He was resurrected, assigned a name (after giving up a reputation) above every name (exalted), given authority (where once He was slave and bondservant), and established as Lord over all.

Until you are willing to step down and take the way of the cross, you are not able to step up, walk in authority, represent His Name, or gain a wholesome reputation and bring glory to the Father. He will raise you up and make your life significant if, and when, you choose His way rather than your own way. And I guarantee that it will not occur at your convenience, but at His. You can be "in the grave" for more than three days.

My life has been broken more than once and poured out like a jar that fell and lost all its precious substance: pride has no place in building the Kingdom of God. If we want more of God, we must be willing to have the Lord remove more of us. If we want to do His thing, our thing must be stripped from us. Unfortunately, we hold so tightly to our life that the process of humiliation can be a messy one.

We may feel, like Moses, that we have nothing left to offer, simply to find that we are now the most usable. When we have come to an end of ourselves, we come to a beginning in Him. When we face our greatest sense of inability, we find that His grace and ability becomes our sufficiency.

Discipline #3

Position Yourself.... Under Spiritual Authority

Listen to what Jesus said about this daily discipline:

"I have never spoken on My own authority or of My own accord or self-appointed, but the Father Who has sent Me has Himself given Me orders on what to say and what to tell. And I know that His commandment is (means) eternal life. So whatever I speak, I am saying [exactly] what My Father has told me to say and in accordance with His instructions" (Jn 12.49-50, AMP).

Scripture affirms that Jesus had to "learn obedience through what He suffered" (Heb 5.8). Do you believe that your training will be any different? Paul's testimony concerning Christ was that submission to His Father's authority resulted in His being given authority by the Father. The resurrection of Jesus made Him "both Christ and Lord" (Ac 2.36). He was exalted above all and given a Name ("Lord") that is respected as an authority in three realms: "in heaven and on earth and under the earth" (Php 2.10-11).

Proverbs warns us to guard our heart with all vigilance, for out of it flows the springs of life (Pr 4.23). Heart motivations, the hidden agendas, attitudes, reactions—these are the stuff of real character! We must learn to exercise spiritual authority over the hidden man of the heart, learn to bring down the giants within, and restore order to the private world before real spiritual authority will be given to us.

The kingdom of self must capitulate (surrender) to the Lordship of Jesus Christ. Self is public enemy number one when it comes to establishing the kingdom of God in our lives. True revival requires death to self. William Law made this statement: "Self is the root, the branches, the tree of all the evils of our fallen state!" In his book Born Crucified, L.E. Maxwell penned these thoughts:

> "God says that the tree must be cut down and uprooted, and left to die, not merely trimmed back. Self-pity, self-righteousness, self-vindication, self-esteem, self-glory—these and ten-thousand other manifestations of the self-life, fleshly foliage ... To trim back only means that the very life of self will go deeper underground, develop more rugged roots and develop into a more vigorous tree."

> **Self can never overcome self.**

Self can never overcome self. Every individual must come to a point where he or she chooses, of their own volition, to end self-control and come under godly authority. Self must die for God's purposes to be revealed and kingdom power to be released into our life. When George Mueller was requested to reveal the secret of his spiritual success, he said:

> "There was a day when I died ... died to George Mueller, his opinions, preferences, tastes, and will; died to the world, its approval or censure; died to the approval or blame even of my brethren and friends; and since then I have studied only to show myself approved unto God."

Before Saul became the Apostle Paul, he had to face the inherent authority of God on the road to Damascus. Watchman Nee stated, "Before a man can subject himself to God's delegated authority, he must first meet up with God's inherent authority... Before [he] can work for God, he must be overturned by His authority" (*Spiritual Authority,* page 13). Because Paul experienced God's authority over him, it was so much easier for him to yield to God's authority in others like Ananias in Acts 9.

It is imperative every purpose-led person knows how to find God's authority in any sphere they are assigned to, honour that authority, serve the vision that is already there, and permit God to raise them up into positions of authority and influence. God requires faithfulness in serving what belongs to another before He entrusts you with your own (Lu 16.12).

One day you will be leading people. You will reap either submission or rebellion that you have sown toward leaders God placed over you (Heb 17). If you want God's assignments to go smoothly in your life, go and find God's authority figures for your life, get into right relationship to them, honour the spirit of authority, learn to obey, experience someone saying "no" to you, and permit God to train you up in being part of the construction gang and not the wrecking crew.

Discipline #4
Speak Wisely

The Bible makes it clear that the way we speak either opens up destiny for us or closes doors. This principle is illustrated in Number 14.2 when Israel complained against leadership and the Lord. Their unholy speech kept them out of the land that God had given them to possess: "So tell them, 'As surely as I live, declares the LORD, I will do to you the very things I heard you say'" (verse 28, NIV). Later on Moses was not allowed to personally take possession of the land because of his reaction to the people, not his disobedience to God (Nu 20.10-12).

Scripture is replete with a description of sins related to the unwise use of the tongue. James makes it clear that the tongue has the potential to set on fire the entire course or cycle of human nature: out of the abundance of the heart the mouth speaks (Lu 6.45); faith comes by hearing what is said even from your own mouth (Ro 10.17); and what is said re-enters and trains the heart, bringing either life or death (Pr 18.21).

Thinking defines us! Not our gifting, our education and intelligence, our friends or our outward appearance, but the way we think! It identifies who we really are. It is not who anyone else says we are (our parents, teachers, friends, boss, or critics) that determines our identity, but who God says we are.

There are some Christians that have demonic strongholds residing within them. Ed Silvoso defined these strongholds as "a mind set impregnated with hopelessness that accepts as unchangeable something that is contrary to the will of God." If we are going to be effective in fulfilling our life assignments, all demonic strongholds must be torn down and rebuilt in Christ (2Co 10.3-5).

> **The way we speak either opens up destiny for us or closes doors.**

The origin of our thoughts must be challenged, the power of those thoughts must be discerned, and the potential or future of those thoughts must be considered seriously. Every thought that we have has a spiritual origin, has the power to affect the now, and the possibility of impacting or impeding our potential or our future.

Our hearts direct our course more than we realize. Proverbs 16.9 says, "A man's heart plans his way." We are instructed to "keep (guard) our heart with all diligence for out of it springs the issues of life" (Pr 4.23). Like a gardener who watches his field, so a man must watch his heart. If a man's heart is larger than his life, his life will be enlarged: if his heart is small, his life will be diminished accordingly. Brian Houston said: "If you think His thoughts, you will have His future" (Jer 29.11-14).

Purpose-led individuals think God's thoughts, speak His Word, feel His emotions, and live out His intentions. It starts with renewing the mind; it ends with a transformed life (Ro 12.1-2). To be a

Life Purpose

transforming influence, one must be renewed to God's way of thinking and speaking. Jesus said, "A good man out of the good treasure of his heart brings forth good things" (Mt 12.35a). What kind of treasure do you have in your heart?

2 Corinthians 4.7 says that "we possess—say, *'I possess!'*"—this precious treasure in [frail, human] vessels of earth, that the grandeur and exceeding greatness of the power may be shown to be of God and not from ourselves" (AMP). "The outlook we have in life is determined by what we are looking out from." Our inner viewpoint (or, treasure) determines our outlook. We cannot separate people's outward function from their inward. Whatever is going on within the private world of the heart and mind is what will soon be exposed in the public world of words and actions.

Get in touch with the treasure within—Christ Himself! What fills your heart? Ralph Waldo Emerson once stated, "What lies behind us and what lies before us are tiny matters as compared to what lies within us."

Our tongue does not have to be a world of iniquity, a death-bringing poison, or a restless evil. Our speech can be changed by the power of God! In Isaiah Chapter 6 we read about God's call upon his life. One of the first things God did was "touch his lips with a coal off the altar." God said, "Your iniquity is taken from you and your sin is completely forgiven." Then Isaiah went forth preaching to a nation, speaking the Word of the Lord, words of truth, but words of love and hope. David wrote, "Whoso offers praise glorifies Me; and to him that orders his conversation aright will I show the salvation of God" (Ps 50.23).

How we speak and the words we speak are really critical disciplines in God's boot camp: the way we handle our speech will either "make a way" or "get in the way" of our destiny and the enjoyment of our inheritance. It will either build or limit our lives. Remember, every word we say either builds up or tears down. Every word we say makes a draw upon our faith or is a response to fear. For every word we say, we will be held accountable. Every word has power to work good or evil. Every word we release will bear fruit that we will eat.

> *"If you don't want to eat of the fruit of sin, stay out of the orchard."*

Discipline #5
A Holy Walk

One of the most notable tragedies of Church history is the reoccurring story of men and women who were mightily used of God, passionately pursued His purposes, fell into sin, and were sidelined from the front lines of ministry. What a sad thing it is to see called, gifted, and appointed people lose the anointing because they couldn't resist temptation.

The Apostle Paul writes to Timothy and gives clarity to the Church:

Life Purpose

"The firm foundation [laid by] God stands, sure and unshaken, bearing this seal (inscription): The Lord knows those who are His, and, let everyone who names [himself by] the name of the Lord give up all iniquity and stand aloof from it (2Ti 2.19-22a, AMP)."

Do you want to be fit and ready for any good work or assignment? Then keep yourself from sin—walk holy before God and man. God loves the sinner, but He still hates sin; therefore, the consequences have not changed—"the wages of sin is still death" (Ro 6.23). Unrepented sin will still lead the sinner into death (Greek thanatos).

Like a piece of wood in a pond, a Christian can "float" (so to speak) on the surface of sin and still not get too wet. But, just as wood that is in the water for any prolonged length of time gets waterlogged and sinks to the bottom, so does the Christian who spends too much time sinning. An older brother in the Lord once gave me this wise advise: "If you don't want to eat of the fruit of sin, stay out of the orchard."

James made it very clear: God doesn't tempt anyone with evil. We are drawn into evil by our own evil thoughts and uncrucified desires; acting on these will cause us to conceive sin; and, acts of sin lead to death (Jas 1.13-16). We are warned not to be misled about this! Galatians 6.7-8 says that "what ever a man sows, that shall he reap: if you sow to the flesh, you will reap destruction; if you sow to the Spirit, you will reap life everlasting."

There are consequences to sinning:

- the discipline of the Lord (Heb 12.4-8)
- a loss of the joy of our salvation (Ps 51.12)
- a loss of fellowship with God (Nu 14.4-44)
- unanswered prayers (Isa 59.1-3)
- generational impact (Ex 20.5-6; King David's sin: 2Sa 12)
- a loss of inheritance (Israel: Heb 3.19–4.1; Esau: 12.15-17)
- undermines our witness (Ro 2.23-24)
- creates spiritual confusion (2Pe 2.20-22)
- loss of the confidence of God (such as Samson; David)

The root of true holiness is an overwhelming passion for the one true and holy God, not for rules, not even principles and standards. The essence of holy living is loving God. People find it easier to serve religion than to build a relationship with God. The holiness that keeps us from sinning must be based upon relationship. We honor those we love.

> **We will learn, in time, when to fight and when to flee.**

This holiness can be seen in Joseph's response to Potiphar's wife as he faced daily temptations to sin against God, another man, and his own life destiny by yielding to adultery (an affair). Joseph wisely said to Potiphar's wife: "How can I do this great evil and sin

Life Purpose

against God?" (Ge 39.9). It was out of his love for God and knowing that sinning against God would affect his destiny that caused Joseph to turn and run.

Every one of God's maturing people will continue to face temptation. We will learn, in time, when to fight and when to flee. Because of our own weaknesses and immaturity, there are times when we must choose flight if we are to avoid sinning and losing destiny. We need to resist the devil and flee to God. Focusing on sin, either by committing it or being consumed with fighting it, keeps us from practicing His Presence. Our relationship becomes based upon what we didn't do rather than upon what we did do.

Sinning is always choosing the wrong choice. However, if we sin, cooperation with the Lord helps us not to repeat it. There is always a sense of failure in yielding to any temptation, but the humiliation that occurs as a result can bring success out of a very terrible situation. We sometimes feel closest to God after we have blown it big time and, in turn, experience true sorrow. Writer Thomas a Kempis commented in *The Imitation of Christ* that he found great potential for growth in every temptation: "Temptations are often very profitable to us, though they may be troublesome and grievous; for in them a man is humbled, purified, and instructed."

Holiness is not based upon the outward appearance or the external expression of Christianity, but it is based entirely upon the attitude of the heart. It is very easy for a man or woman to refrain from adultery, but it may not be as easy to refrain from glances of the eyes, from uttering or listening to flattery, and so on. Holiness is not built upon the repression of evil, concentrated on what one can not do, but on doing what pleases God. Holiness is submission to His work being formed within us, before it is "doing good works for Him."

Sin creates massive disturbances in our lives; holiness brings peace. Sin is not inviting, but debilitating; holiness is not burdensome, but liberating. Anything God wills is good and right for us, and anything He does not will is bad and wrong. There is no gray area: no fence line to sit on.

The less conscious the Christian is to sin in his own life, the less conscious the unbeliever will be to sin within society. When Christians become Christian, the world has the chance to become Christian. The Church must walk holy: when it does, it can justifiably rebuke the world of sin; when it does not, who then can rebuke the world?

In his book *Sanctification, Experience and Ethics*, R.T. Williams made this insightful statement:

> "Offer the world a religion it can take along with its sinful pleasures and the following will be many. However, when you ask men to die to sin and surrender their wills to God, to give up their own plans and their own ambitions and their own philosophy of life and take Jesus and what He has to offer, you begin a battle that determines the outcome and destiny of souls, the religion that demands denial of self

has never been popular and it can never be popular . . . a religion that comes into conflict with the human heart will immediately meet opposition."

God has not called us to impurity but to consecration (1Th 4.7)—to excel at living a God-pleasing life (God's Word). We should pursue what has God's approval: holiness. It's the only way to go.

> *"A religion that comes into contact with the human heart will meet opposition."*
> R.T. Williams

Discipline #6
Give the Gift Away

Every one of us has been graced and gifted by God. Paul speaks of "having gifts according to the grace that is given to us" (Ro 12.6). All of these gifts originate with God: they come from Him and they return to Him. We all have something someone else needs, and we all have a need and a seed to sow.

The gifts outlined in scripture are leadership gifts (Eph 4); ministry gifts (Ro 12); and spiritual gifts (1Co 12).

God makes it clear that these gifts are irrevocable. Once given to you and invested into your life, they will never be withdrawn (Ro 11.29). God will not change His mind because He didn't make a mistake. What He requires is simple: "Each one should use whatever gift he has received to serve others, faithfully administering God's grace in its various forms (1Pe 4.10, NIV).

These gifts are unique and diverse (1Co 12.4). God requires a proper stewardship of the gift: use the gift and the gift will grow; bury the gift and it may diminish! Paul writes in 1 Corinthians 4.2: "It is required in stewards that a man be found faithful." It is vital that all "seek to excel to the edifying of the church" (1Co 14.12).

God asked Moses, "What is in your hand?" (Ex 4.2). With the rod in his hand, Moses was able to lead a nation into their freedom. Elisha asked the widow, "What is in your house?" (2Ki 4). She replied: "Only a pot of oil." But when she stewarded that oil, God enabled her and her family to live off a miracle for many years.

What are you doing with what you have been given? This is the question. Unless we are sowing the gift God has given us and serving others, it is improbable that God will activate it on our behalf when He needs it. He will be looking for someone who is faithfully using what has been invested in them. Scripture makes it clear that those who hide it may get a rebuke, not a nod of approval (Mt 25).

Mike Murdoch made a profound statement. He said, and I believe it, "What you are willing to make happen for others, God will make happen for you!" If you sow your gifts to make someone else's vision succeed, I am convinced that God will bring people into your life who will sow their gifts into your life to help you succeed. You will need the gifts of others when you are on assignment: sow your gifts now, and you will reap later on from many sources.

Discipline #7
Be A Fighter

One of the most perplexing scenarios I have watched over the years has been the blatant willingness of some people to let their pastors or counselors fight for aspects of their life that they should be fighting for. Sometimes I have voiced what I felt and said to married couples: "It appears to me that I want this marriage to work more than you want it to work!" All too often it was the truth.

There is an enemy. We are at war. There are real casualties, real victories, and real defeats. There are causes worth fighting for (1Sa 17.9). There are times when you must put your faith on the line. There are occasions when turning and fleeing is not the answer, when there is no excuse for compromise, when retreat would mean the destruction of a future. The will to take a stand and not be moved is critical.

Every assignment from heaven has an enemy! Look what happened when Saul was converted and then went preaching in the synagogues: the Jews conspired to kill him (Ac 9.23). Every dream from God has a dream killer! Look what happened to

Joseph when he verbalized the dream to his brothers (Ge 37.19-20). The enemy's reaction can be a tool in the Lord's Hand to confirm to us we are on the right road, doing the right thing.

> *If we are willing to fight, our enemy will, in fright, break into flight.*

The Lord is our Champion! He has given us weapons of war so that we can successfully stand up against the deceptive tactics of the enemy and fulfill the will of God (Eph 6.10-18). These weapons are His weapons: His truth, His righteousness, His salvation, His peace, His Word, His Spirit, His faith. We have been outfitted with the armor of light—His armor (Ro 13.12). We can make a successful defense of our faith against the enemy: if we are willing to fight, our enemy will, in fright, break into flight (Jas 4.7).

Discipline #8
Develop Unbreakable, Godly Friendships

When I was a youth pastor I introduced a motto to our youth group from Winkey Pratney's book *Youth Aflame* on how we should live our lives. It went like this: "We will no longer follow a multitude to do evil, but we are determined to do the will of God in all things, no matter what the world thinks or says about us."

Life Purpose

This statement became an integral part in helping me to be the person I am today. It helped me to stand my ground when others fell away. It helped me to stand for righteousness when others opted for compromise. It helped me to speak out when others were deathly quiet. It helped me to develop a life that was based upon conviction, rather than preference.

If you want God to employ you in His company, you must be willing to clean-up compromising relationships. Listen to the Message Translation of James 4.6-10:

> "You're cheating on God. If all you want is your own way, flirting with the world every chance you get, then you end up enemies of God and His way. And do you suppose God doesn't care? The proverb has it that 'He's a fiercely jealous lover.' And what He gives in love is always far better than anything else you'll find. It is common knowledge that 'God goes against the willful proud; God gives grace to the willing humble.' So let God work His will in you. Yell a loud 'no' to the devil and watch him scamper. Say a quiet 'yes' to God and He'll be there in no time. Quit dabbling in sin. Purify your inner life. Quit playing the field. Hit bottom and cry your eyes out. The fun and games are over. Get serious, really serious. Get down on your knees before the Master; it's the only way you'll get on your feet."

Scripture says that "a man that hath friends must shew himself friendly: and there is a friend that sticketh closer than a brother" (Pr 18.24, KJV); "friends come and friends go, but a true friend sticks by you like family" (TMT). The Bible describes Jesus as a "friend (Greek philos-friendly) of even publicans (tax collectors) and sinners" (Mt 11.19).

> **Jesus could love the sinner and not lower his standards.**

Everywhere that Jesus went, He was popular. Men and women sensed His loving concern for them. He showed love to all ages, genders, races, and religious persuasions. His first act was to choose men who would be companions in the cause.

However, and this is key, Jesus could love the sinner and not lower His standards. Love was not a feeling to Jesus; it was a moral choice. He was under His Father's command to love people! Loving people and befriending people was an act of obedience, as well as a joy.

Christ's refusal to lower His standards also brought Him great persecution and cut Him off from many of His friends; for example, he was lonely, but not a loner. There were few people He did not offend; for instance, his mother ("I must be about my father's business"); disciples (Jn 6); friends like Lazarus; religious leaders (ready to kill Him), and so forth. Jesus was not afraid to stand alone because of His convictions. His only intent was to obey the Father's will at all cost.

Life Purpose

Coming to Christ costs you something—everything, inclusive of family and friends (Lu 14.26). Paul faced that cost at the end of his life when many of his friends deserted him and he had to stand alone (2Ti 4.16). You can be assured that God will restore to you all that you give up for Him and for the gospel's sake (Mk 10.28-30).

Life and death is at stake in all of our relationships, the choice of our friendships. Friends can take you to heaven; fiends can take you to hell. Your destiny in life is intricately connected to who you recognize and listen to as your friend. So God has a great interest in who you count as your friends, for friendship with ungodly people will ultimately change them or you! There is a line of influence that must be watched quite diligently because it entertains and plays with life and death.

The Psalmist said: "Blessed is the man who walks and lives not in the counsel of the ungodly (following their advice, plans and purposes), nor stands (submissive and inactive) in the path where sinners walk, nor sits down (to relax and rest) where the scornful (and the mockers) gather" (Ps 1.1).

The wisdom writer said: "My son, if sinners entice you, do not consent. If they say 'Come with us—restrain your foot from their path'" (Pr 1).

If you listen to wisdom, God promises that you will "be delivered from evil men . . . men who forsake the paths of righteousness . . . who delight in the perverseness of evil, who are crooked in their ways, devious in their paths" (Pr 2.12-15).

The world is after your heart. Who you let into your heart will have its affect on you for life. In Proverbs, the adulterous woman is spoken of as having feet that go down to death (Pr 5.5). "Can a man take fire to his bosom and not be burned?" (Pr 6.27). So, "keep and guard your heart with all vigilance, for out of it flows the springs of life" (Pr 4.23).

Here is some biblical wisdom:

- Proverbs 13.20: "He who walks [as a companion] with
- wise men shall be wise, but he who associates with
- [self-confident] fools will [be a fool himself and] shall smart for it" (AMP).
- Proverbs 22.24-25: "Make no friendships with a man given to anger, and with a wrathful man do not associate, lest you learn his ways and get yourself into a snare" (AMP).
- Proverbs 27.17: "Iron sharpens iron; so a man sharpens the countenance of his friend [to show rage or worthy purpose] (AMP) . . . and your face mirrors your heart" (TMT).
- 1 Corinthians 15.33: "Do not be deceived and misled! Evil companionships corrupt (Greek phtheiro—ruin, spoil) and deprave good manners and morals and character" (AMP).

You gotta know who is a God designed relationship for your life.

Life Purpose

Your choice of friends determines direction and destiny! Lot "pitched his tent toward Sodom" and chose the people of Sodom over his own uncle, Abraham, and it cost him his family, home, and his business—he saved his skin, but lost his kin (Ge 13). Samson hung out with the wrong woman, Delilah, and it cost him his natural and spiritual vision. He also lost his life in the process (Jdg 16). It matters who gives you a haircut.

Balaam put his prophetic gift out for sale to a foreign king and it cost him his life (Nu 22–24); Peter stood and warmed himself around a fire with the wrong people and it caused him to deny he ever knew the Lord (Jn 18.25); and Judas connected with the wrong group and he betrayed Christ.

Some of the best intentions in friendships have led to some of the greatest crimes against humanity. You gotta know who is a God-designed relationship for your life.

Let's face it! It is really important that every one of your relationships be reviewed in the light of His standards, not your own. The way of the crowd is usually the wrong way! If you are going to go God's way, you are going to lose some friendships. If you are going to serve Jesus, you have to give up the opinions and the applause of the "in crowd."

Mike Murdoch stated, "When God wants to bless you, He brings a person into your life; when the enemy wants to destroy you, he brings a person into your life!" It is, therefore, extremely critical that you discern the people who are crossing your spiritual path.

Your real Christianity is exposed in how you talk about Jesus or stand for moral positions around your friends, the people that you really care about, and who should care for you! What do you do when you are in an environment where it is a reproach to be called a Christian? Will you go all out for Christ or deny Him before the world?

Unholy alliances destroy people as well as nations. Unless they are permanently broken, it will lead you into a conspiracy with darkness, an alignment with evil that will draw you in spiritually. Tolerating wrong, allowing mockery, permitting détente, compromising on moral positions will lead you into the ditch and bring your life under judgment with the world.

Trust the Holy Spirit. He knows how to convict us about improper relationships! Be open to watchman God has placed around us, watching over our souls. They are there to guard us from falling back from the grace of God and becoming defiled and contaminated by the deceitfulness of sin (Heb 3.12-13). It is necessary that we repent of and break free from any kind of corrupting influence.

Life Purpose

Discipline #9
Freely You Have Received, Freely Give!

God is looking for someone who will work with Him and believe and obey! It's not just a duty or a responsibility but a privilege: obedience becomes a joy, not a law! He has made our faith a determining factor! He won't go any further than we are willing to go. Therefore, we must position ourselves to believe and partner with Him.

> **God is a giver; not a taker.**

When you accept an assignment, you will need to know about God's provision. I believe that what I sow towards another's Kingdom initiatives, I will reap towards that which God has called me to do. Proverbs 11. 24-25 states: "One man gives freely, yet gains even more; another withholds unduly, but comes to poverty. A generous man will prosper; he who refreshes others will himself be refreshed" (NIV). When you are His servant, obeying His Word, walking in His will, and favouring His righteous cause, it it His desire to prosper you. He does that by teaching you to give away what you have.

God is a giver—not a taker! He gave His Son. When you were born, He gave you life (Ps 139). Now He asks that you act, as He did, and give your life away as well! "Give, and it will be given to you. A good measure, pressed down, shaken together and running over, will be poured into your lap. For with the measure you use, it will be measured to you" (Lu 6.38, NIV).

God wants you operating with a supernatural surplus. But that will require, on your part, a willingness to put His wealth into circulation. It is imperative that we press past giving out of greed, motivated by need to do a great deed, and start seeing our giving as sowing seed!

He has already provided us with the seed: it is mandatory that we return it to Him by investing into Kingdom initiatives (Mal 3.8-10) that will open up wide to us the window of heaven and determine the devourer's attempts to impoverish us. There is a caution, however, because Deuteronomy 8.18 says, "But remember the LORD your God, for it is He who gives you the ability to produce wealth, and to confirm His covenant" (NIV).

Over and above giving leads to over and above living. Over and above sowing must match our over and above saying! Talking about blessing must be preceded with reaching out and blessing. It's harvest time all over the world: I want to be involved in taking in the harvest, one of the most expensive times of the whole process. There is a price to pay.

Isaiah 32.20 says: "Happy and fortunate are you who cast your seed upon all waters [when the river overflows its banks; for the seed will sink into the mud and when the waters subside will spring up; you

Life Purpose

will find it after many days in an abundant harvest]" (AMP).
You make the decision: it has to do with attitude. Are you going to give—please check:

- ☐ Sparingly or bountifully (2Co 9.6).
- ☐ Out of selfishness (giving to get to keep) or out of sufficiency (giving to get to give again).
- ☐ From the flesh (led by personal agenda) or by the Spirit (led by God's agenda) (Gal 6.7-10).
- ☐ Out of a poverty spirit (complaining you don't have enough) or out of a prosperous spirit (I have more than enough to be a blessing).
- ☐ For the blessing (and recognition) of man or for the blessing (and praise) of the Lord (Pr 10.22).
- ☐ Serving mammon (the way the world uses resources) or serving God (directing them God's way) (Mt 6.24).
- ☐ Your first fruits or your last fruits (Pr 3.9).
- ☐ Because you have to (coercion) or ought to (obligation) orwant to (delight and joy to bless) (Lu 11.42; Mt 23.23).
- ☐ A tip (if you think He or His church deserves it) or a tithe (a tenth of your income) or a gift (recognizing that God owns and has the right to ask for it all) (1Co 16.1-2).
- ☐ Out of need—when you see it out of greed—for what you want to get out of it or because you want to seed—you want to be a part of seeing potential realized, dreams come into reality, and prophetic vision come to pass.

God has a way of making less more when we invest in His Kingdom initiatives. He also has a way of making more less when we keep it and spend it on ourselves. Giving tests our faith, and it also tests our faithfulness. Can we believe that God will take less and make it more? The spirit of poverty says: "Don't lose what you have!" The spirit of mammon says: "You are going to need everything you have," adding fear, greed, and worry into the mix. God says, "Prove Me now and see if I will not open the windows of heaven and pour out a blessing that there shall not be room enough to receive it" (Mal 3.10, KJV).

You have got to break out in your spirit concerning giving before you will ever break out in fulfilling His purpose for your life. I can guarantee that the time will come where your needs will be greater than your apparent provision and you will have only one confidence to hold on to: "I have honoured the Lord with my giving and sown to see His will accomplished, and He will honour me now and provide all that I need and more."

I have travelled worldwide on mission assignments. There has not been one nation that I have ministered into that God has not first asked me to sow towards before I ever put one foot on its soil. One year my family put our money together to buy Bibles for Fiji instead of Christmas presents for each other.

Two years later, my wife and I and Brodie, my oldest (at that time, five years of age), spent six weeks ministering in Fiji. One day we were taken to minister

Life Purpose

in some villages around Savu Savu. We were greeted with such honour and love. Later I found out why: our names were in the Bibles in their hands. Our gift had preceded us and made a way for ministry. I believe that when we give, we are sowing into the future lives of other people and our own future.

> **"Most people don't resist change, they resist being changed."**
> (Anonymous)

Chapter 19

Master Keys

"Life is like a can of sardines. We are, all of us, looking for the right key."

Alan Bennet

"Find a thing that you love to do and you will never have to work a day in your life."

Harvey MacKay

A lighthouse keeper who worked on a rockystretch of coastline received his new supply of oil once a month to keep the light burning. Not being far from shore, he had frequent guests who requested to use some of his oil. Since all the requests seemed legitimate, the lighthouse keeper tried to please everyone and grant the requests of all. Toward the end of the month he noticed that his supply of oil had dwindled drastically. Soon it was gone, and the beacon went out. That night several ships were wrecked and lives were lost. When the authorities investigated, the man was very repentant. To his excuses and pleading their reply was, "You

Life Purpose

were given oil for one purpose—to keep that light burning."

John Maxwell
Developing the Leader Within You (page 25)

I have not always loved keys. The fewer the better. I am known in my home for losing my keys. My problem is I tend to blame other people for moving my keys and then placing them somewhere other than where I thought I had placed them. Those keys are critical to the success of my day: they get me into my car and start it up; they open my office doors; they help me to re-enter my home after a long day at work. I don't need a lot of keys: I just need the right key, in the right place, at the right time.

I have come to love master keys. They do not just open one door: they open them all. I believe that the Bible is filled with Master keys—thoughts, perspectives, challenges, concepts, ideas—that will open up your life to next steps. The right key can open your future in amazing ways.

Master keys give you clues to your life purpose. I am very convinced that they will bring clarity to next steps in your life. They will help you to be successful in making movement towards the purpose God has planned and scheduled in your life's journey. Sooner or later, the pieces of the puzzle will cause your life to make sense. The dots will connect, so to speak, and you will get His picture for your life.

Have fun with the exercise below. It will provide you with some interesting questions, that, if answered thoughtfully and honestly, may provide some keys and clues into the next steps of your life's journey.

What's In A Name?

There is often a spiritual significance to the meaning of your name. What does your name mean? You are called by your name every day. My name, David, means *"beloved of the Lord."* The significance of that name is being driven home every time I hear it. Names are often chosen for a specific reason. They often reflect, sooner or later, a gifting or express a personality. They are also subject to change by conversion: for example, Jacob ("supplanter") to Israel ("contender with God").

When Saul was converted he had a mission change and charge to reach the Gentiles with the Gospel: his name was changed to Paul to open those doors. We know him as Paul, his Greek name. Scripture says that we are all going to be given a new name (Rev 2.17). I personally believe that our names will be representative of our character, our call, and our gifts: the name we are given will reveal all about us.

When I go to Taipei, Taiwan, I stay in the home of some lovely Chinese Christians. They have been deeply involved with leaders from Crossroads, YWAM for many years. Her name is Jingle and her husband's name is Bell. Both of them bring a great deal of joy to everyone. When I was sharing this concept, I asked

Life Purpose

her what her name means. She shared that it means she was a port of call, where ships entered a nation, deposited their goods, and left. They have been doing exactly that for many ministries and the idea that she was living out the name she was given brought her great joy.

I am especially attracted to the Chinese nations. I believe one of the reasons my heart has been drawn to them has been the tradition of giving a Christian name to those who have come to know Christ because of the ministry. I have been very privileged to give many Chinese people their Christian name, and I take that very seriously. It has been amazing to me, upon my return to their homeland, to see them living out their name and to see the key it has given them for their life purpose.

A Genogram

Generational influences can have an affect on who we are today and what we believe we can become, both positively and negatively. Take a look at your ancestry and make a note of incidences and influences upon your life and your family. Write down and evaluate all of the predominating sins or blessings. If there are negative events and influences, have they been brought to the cross? If there are positive events and influences, are you aware of the grace that is upon you to help you fulfill your destiny?

Both positive and negative generational influences must be yielded to God. Remember, they are simply influences, not controlling forces. Take the positive influences and sanctify those strengths for the work God has prepared for you. Sin may have its effect up to the third or fourth generation, but grace and righteousness will have its effect up to a thousand generations (Ex 20.4).

We are all a composite of generational influences. There are spirits that attach themselves to sin: for instance, Abraham, Isaac, and Jacob had to deal with issues of deceitfulness and preferential treatment of their children. Those tendencies were broken in the life of Joseph. You can break the curse of sin through prayer and the blood of Christ.

The Holy Spirit also gives witness and a transgenerational blessing on the righteous. Second and third generation Christians do not have to get lethargic and indifferent to the Gospel: they can draw upon a double anointing which is the impartation of the righteous. They can gratefully receive the joy and blessing that is passed down through righteousness and know that those blessings—memories, gifts, anointings, callings, graces—will be used to help fulfill your life purpose.

Specific Scriptures, Quotations, and Prophetic Words

Purpose-filled people have a sense of calling. That usually means a drawing to a specific verse or

Life Purpose

verses of scripture. Five years ago while I was sitting in the Dallas Convention Center in Texas, listening to Dr. Brown pray after a wonderful session on revival and the apostolic, I asked the Lord for a word to help me see with clarity the next phase of my ministry. Dr. Brown interrupted the closing prayer and spoke this word from Romans 1.5 to *"someone out there."* "It is through Him that [you] have received grace—God's unmerited favour—and (your) apostleship to promote obedience to the faith and make disciples for His Name's sake among all the nations" (AMP). That word has taken me to many nations around the world and become a mission statement for my life.

We all need sealed orders. There are reasons why you are attracted to specific scriptures: they have something to say about what you are supposed to do in life. Do you have a life purpose mission statement? There are reasons certain quotes or sayings stick in your mind. There are reasons why certain prophetic words have been given over you: don't despise them. They have a time of fulfillment (Hab 2.1-4): they confirm the steps of the righteous.

I was again asking the Lord a number of years ago about next steps. I attended a prophetic conference at my close friend Pastor Wes Campbell's church in Kelowna. My son, Brodie and I were chosen out of the crowd. I was given a word that the Lord was opening Asia up to me in ministry. I went home and prayed over that word and three weeks later I received three confirming calls to minister into Asian countries.

Listen to the source of the words given. Honour the Lord and give Him time to confirm to your heart His word. Don't forget them: pull them out and read them occasionally. Bring to remembrance what the Lord has given you and pray over them. Sooner or later, if they are true words, they will come to pass and become part of the confirming and empowering tools of the Lord to get you from where you are to where He wants you to be.

Mentors

We all need discernment about the people who are influencing our lives. If you give authority to any relationships that are not godly, their destiny may become yours.

Abraham was a very positive influence on Lot's life. When Lot separated from Abraham, his life took a downward turn. He almost lost everything. There are some people we need to disconnect from, but there are also some relationships we must value and hold close to. They will help us get to the place where God is waiting with our next marching orders.

What individual(s) has had the greatest impact upon your life, living or dead? If alive, do they know? Do you know why? There will be something about their life that is attractive to you for a reason. That reason is a clue into your life purpose. God always provides models to help us get to the next level, or to move us into next assignments.

Life Purpose

If there are none, are there people whose lives you would like to imitate, who you believe would help you to become your very best and reach your full potential in God? Ask yourself, "If I could work for anybody, for somebody doing something in particular, who would that be, what would I do and why?"

Books

Books, authors, biographies, and specific speakers that we will sacrifice to hear all make an indelible impression on our lives. If you looked at your library, what kinds of books are you attracted to? If your library is strong on spiritual warfare themes, it is possible that is a clue into your calling or gifting. What you are being equipped in is often a precursor to what you will be used in.

What biographies have moved you? Why? Have you ever pondered why some people's lives have so motivated you? Possibly they are biographies of missionaries: are you being prepared for missions work? Maybe they are stories about businessmen and their adventures in the corporate world: is God preparing you to become a financier of the Great Commission? I am confident that your research into these influential people and stories will provide a clue into what you are being prepared to accomplish.

When I first started my youth ministry, I felt led to take our youth group through a three-year study into Watchman Nee's complete work on The Spiritual Man. It had a profound impact upon the group, many of whom went on to become Christian leaders with a good foundation as to who they are in Christ. I do not advise every youth pastor to do the same.

However, years later, while preaching through a Chinese translator in Taipei, I was told that the translators found it easy to translate my teaching. God had prepared me for ministry to the Chinese people twenty years earlier by giving me a crash course in Watchman Nee's theology. Only He knew I was going to need it one day.

Your Passion

Life assignments are often linked to emotions or passions of the heart. In Christ's ministry, He was moved with compassion and miracles followed. By tracking "what moves us," we may be able to gain ownership to another clue or key to our destiny. "What bothers you the most? What makes you angry enough for you to rise up inside with a desire to see something change? What grieves your spirit or violates your convictions?"

Those people or circumstances that agitate an emotional response are usually people to whom you have been assigned, or circumstances you have been called upon to influence. I just love the statement Bob Beckett made: *"If you want to make an impact, you must be committed to having a collision."*

What obsesses you? What are you constantly thinking and talking about? This creates desire within you! What draws upon your compassion, or awakens

Life Purpose

your energy to get involved? The Bible says that "Jesus, for the joy that was set before Him, endured the cross" (Heb 12.2, KJV). We are what Jesus was all about—He was thinking about us! We are His joy that helped Him endure the cross—we are worth more to Him than the pain and disgrace of the cross. He set His eyes and walk and did not draw back from His mission (Isa 50.7).

What joy is set before you? You will be remembered for what grabbed a hold of your heart—your passion (Ps 69.9). God also brings people of similar passions into your life to help you walk the journey together and to fulfill the assignments that come from the throne. People only succeed at something they are passionate about.

Does the path you are traveling capture your heart? Is what you are doing something you can give your whole heart, mind, soul, and strength to? God instructs us to be passionate about life: we are to "guard our affections, for they influence everything else in our life" (Pr 4.23, TLB).

When your desire for inheritance is greater than your fear of giants in the land, you can walk into your future and enjoy the blessing of obedience.

Faithfulness in Obedience and Completion

What was the last assignment that God gave to you? Were you willingly obedient to do it? Did you complete what He asked you to do? You will never be ready for the next assignment if you have been unfaithful and negligent in completing previous directives. You can never go beyond your last act of disobedience. Remember the little city of Ai after Jericho (Jos 7)? Even though they won a miraculous victory at Jericho, the nation's lack of obedience closed the door to Ai.

Mike Murdoch has made this statement: "God will never promote you until you have become overqualified for your present assignment." One cannot move to Grade 10 without finishing the homework for Grade 9. Success, Eugene Patterson says is "one long obedience in the same direction." God is on the lookout for faithful, faithful people: Proverbs 20.6 says, "Many a man claims to have unfailing love, but a faithful man who can find?"

If you have disobeyed for one reason or another, failure can be a tool to help you succeed. God can turn your failures into successes, if you will let Him. He knows how to make something beautiful out of ashes (Isa 61.3). With God, failure is only delay, not defeat; a temporary detour, not a dead-end street (William A. Ward). Failure is one of the most powerful laws of success.

Most men have failed before they succeeded at their life purpose. History is kind to recording their failures in view of their personal breakthroughs. We are left with success stories of people who pushed through their own inadequacies and found their strength in God: they failed, but they were not failures; they fell, but they didn't stay down. They fell forward.

Life Purpose

Read through the Apostle Paul's records of his own fears and worries and his attempts to understand what made him get up and run the race—to the finish line—when everything was against him making it (2Co 4.7-12). He had persevered and learned to fail forward into the grace and resurrection power of God. Like Amos, he had found the nerve to say, "Rejoice not against me, O mine enemy: when I fall, I shall arise; when I sit in darkness, the LORD shall be a light unto me" (Mic 7.8).

Elisha was called by Elijah to come and follow him. Elisha persisted in faithfulness when other prophets-in-training checked out. Learn to complete the task. The double portion is at the end of this walk of faithfulness. How long do you remain faithful? As long as it takes to see the impartation come, or the anointing applied to your life for next steps.

Your Uniqueness

Have you spent time trying to understand your uniqueness? What makes you who you are apart from other people? Have you learned to celebrate your uniqueness and the diversity that is found in the relationships God has given you? Don't try to be an echo to your generation when God has raised you up to be a voice.

Stop struggling to be someone else: if you do that, the best you can be is runner-up. If there are two of you, there is no need for one of you. Surely, if God makes no two snowflakes alike, then He has created you to be entirely different for a God-designed intention: the fact that the DNA of our hair is unique or there are no two fingerprints alike, should tell you something.

You don't have to prove your worth to God—you have been "made worthy" (Col 1.12). You must now learn to believe in your value, discern it, and celebrate it. Maybe you are called to a governmental office. What is the main gift that motivates you from Romans 12.3-21? There are many wonderful tools of assessment out there to help you define that. What power gifts are you seeking in prayer, and why have you chosen them? (1Co 12.4-11).

There is someone, somewhere out there waiting for you to emerge. There is but one you: if you do not rise up and become all that God intended you to be and do what he Has called and suited you to do, then who will? Do not permit excuses for neglecting the gift inside you, the treasure that has been wisely invested within (Mt 25.24-25).

Seed who you are. Write down every gift you have, every bit of training you have received, every place you have been, every friend you have, every talent you possess, and sow who you are into those around you. There is enough seed in you to grow a future, if you plant it and give it away. Your seed is the only influence you have upon your future.

Money

"If money was no object and you could do anything that God wanted you to do, and you knew you could not fail, what would you attempt to do for God?" So often money, rather than the will of God, rules our heart's vision. We say, *"I can't,"* so quickly when God is saying, *"You can."* Remove money from the equation of vision for a moment and some light may be shed on your real heart's desires and motivations.

Another way of looking at this may be: "If all of your financial needs were already met, what would you like to spend the rest of your life doing?" If you knew you had all the fiscal support you needed, what would you begin creating? Why would you choose to do that? What is hindering you from starting? Where could you begin right now?

Nothing begins with money: everything begins from the issues of the heart. Proverbs 4.23 says, "Keep vigilant watch over your heart; that's where life starts" (TMT). Find out where your heart is at first: people with money are always attracted to people with passion. You will find that your heart's vision will attract investment monies. Remember, it is always a matter of finding God's will first: there is, as has often been quoted, always "provision for the vision."

Don't allow a lack of finances to stop you from dreaming God's dreams. Most people's fear of failure is caught up with their fear of financial lack. It it essential that God become your greatest partner in every initiative: and, if God is for you, who can be against you? Every great man and woman of God were given divine assignments greater than their resources, and it caused them to trust in One who was greater than any of the potential problems.

David Kalamen

Remember, God will never ask you to do anything that He is not willing to finance, and you will never face any situation that is bigger than God has already thought about and taken into consideration before giving you the assignment. You will need money, but that is not what you need first: you will need to know the will of God. Actively set your heart to receive the abundance of God: His prosperity will be "enough to complete the instructions He has for your life."

> *Give a man a dollar and you cheer his heart.*
> *Give a man a dream and you challenge his heart.*
> *Give him Christ and you change his heart.*
> *Then the dollar and the dream*
> *becomes meaningful to him and to others.*
> C. Neil Strait

Life Purpose

Chapter 20
Cheering On The Church!
"Finish Well"

While I was on a ministry trip in New Zealand quite a number of years ago, I drove by a new housing development. I couldn't help noticing this huge sign at the entrance way into the subdivision. It read, "Finisher's Wanted." This is a Kiwi reference to the construction guys who complete the home once the framing has been completed. There ought to be a sign like that outside every church, every youth rally, and so on. That is what Christ requires from us.

Dean Sherman, YWAM

Kathryn Kuhlman was asked to speak to a graduating class at Oral Roberts University. Her sermon was entitled *Graduation to Glory.* Before Miss Kuhlman began her main message, she gave this little story. She said, "There may be those of you who wonder what my relationship is to Oral Roberts University. I am here today to receive an honourary Doctorate Degree. But I had better declare myself right at the beginning. I have it here in black and white. It was written by one of the greatest sports writers in the United States. 'Oral Roberts, needing a little bit more to go all the way, signed on Kathryn Kuhlman as head cheer leader.' My position with Oral Roberts University is cheerleader. That is a pretty important position, wouldn't you say? I am your head cheerleader!"

In late 2003 I had the privilege of getting to know a precious sister, Dr. Ruth Ruibal. She and her husband, Julio, were called to evangelize the people of South America. In 1978, after years of apostolically ministering throughout the region, they responded to the call of God and settled in Cali, Columbia. Shortly, thereafter, they established Ekklesia Columbian Christian Center. It was here that Julio became a 20th Century martyr. His life was sacrificed for the cause of Christ and for the transformation of his city: he was a modern example of a gentleman who *"gave himself for God's purposes" (Unity in the Spirit,* Ruth Ruibal, dedication page).

I was inspired by Julio's simple devotion to serving the purposes of God in his generation, even if it cost him his life. I wish I had known him. From what I have seen of the family, they, too, carry that same faith and commitment to the cause of the King, and we are becoming friends. The blood of this martyr that fell into the city of Cali's soul and soil has become the rallying call for the City Church to merge and emerge as a force for change.

Life Purpose

Before his death, Julio made this comment: *"I know that I am immortal until I have done all that the Lord has for me to do"* (*Anointed*, Julio C. Ruibal, page 162).

On December 13th, 1995, God's assignment for Julio was completed and he is now in the presence of the Heavenly Father. I am convinced that he is there cheering on the Church to its highest call and destiny.

The Apostle Paul wrote: "He who began a good work in you will perform it" (Php 1.6). The Amplified Bible says that "right up until the time of His return [God] will develop [that good work] and perfect and bring it to full completion in you." We can be confident of this. We are not alone on our journey, and we are not living without His full attention and help. He is the "Author and the Finisher of our faith" (Heb 12.2)—He is the Cause and the Completer, the Pioneer and the Perfecter. God was there at the beginning and He will see us cross the finish line (Zec 4.9).

As Christ was given works to do (Jn 5.36) and He testified that He had completed those works (Jn 17.4), He was able to finish well (Jn 19.30). It is the Father's desire to see every one of us start and finish well. He encourages us not to allow anything or anyone to hinder us from completing the race when we began so well (Gal 5.7).

I have found that true success is letting God be God to you, then letting God be God in you, and then, letting God be God *through* you! The cost of true success is never as high as the cost of failure, and failure will last as long as you permit it (1Co 3.5).

Faith and obedience is the *only* thing God has ever required of us: when we make it our heart to obey Him bringing Him pleasure, He opens up His Heart to bring us pleasure.

What progress are you standing in the way of? Your own? Others? Ten years from now, what will you wish you had done? What is the first small step you can take to get yourself moving in God's direction? "You will never be free until you've been made a captive of God's supreme plan for your life."

I personally believe that a person's boredom in life is in direct proportion to the degree that they are outside the will and plan of God. If you were to rate your degree of boredom, where would you place yourself? What are you going to do about regaining your spiritual passion and zeal and returning to your first love?

What you do with the next thirty days of your life could have a qualitative impact upon your future. Mike Murdoch gave some precise statements that are extremely pertinent to your decision-making process. He said, "Only an intolerance of the present can create a future . . . Whatever you tolerate, you cannot change . . . You have no right to something you are not willing to pursue."

What changes do you feel that you need to make in your life within the next 30 days to better position yourself for God's special assignment? Make a quality decision to get on with the grand purpose of pursuing passionately His presence and His eternal plan. There is no better time to start than the present. God is a

Life Purpose

"*now*" God! When are you going to begin? Every act of obedience is going to provide another step which will bring you closer to that which makes your life significant. It becomes another piece of the puzzle that will make the picture so much clearer and your future so much brighter.

Your destiny is not a matter of chance or luck, but it is a discovery of His will. Your success will depend upon God's empowering grace and your personal decision-making. There is an upward call resting upon your life. May God grace you with the will and the strength to discover this, and may you complete the course He has planned for your life and receive the grand prize. So start training for a marathon, but have enough kick left in you to sprint the final leg of the race. *Exitus probe*—finish well, my friend!

> *In the movie Chariots of Fire, young Harold Abrahams, a champion sprinter, had just suffered his first-ever defeat. When his girlfriend tried to encourage him, he bellowed, "If I can't win, I won't run." To which she wisely replied, "If you don't run, you can't win." Abrahams went on to win the 1924 Olympic Gold Medal in the hundred-meter run.*
> Illustrations for Biblical Preaching (page 263)

David Kalamen

The Martyr's Creed

I am part of the "Fellowship of the Unashamed." The die has been cast. I have stepped over the line. The decision has been made. I am a disciple of Jesus Christ. I won't look back, let up, slow down, back away, or be still. My past is redeemed, the present makes sense, and my future is secure. I am completely finished and done with low living, sight walking, small planning, smooth knees, colourless dreams, chintzy giving, and dwarfed goals.

I no longer need pre-eminence, prosperity, position, promotions, plaudits, or popularity. I now live by presence, lean by faith, love by patience, lift by prayer, and labor by power. My pace is set, my gait is fast, my goal is Heaven, my road is narrow, my way is rough, my companions few, my Guide reliable, my mission clear. I cannot be bought, turned back, compromised, deterred, lured away, diluted, or delayed.

I will not flinch in the face of sacrifice, hesitate in the presence of adversity, negotiate at the table of the enemy, ponder at the pool of popularity, or meander in the maze of mediocrity.

I am a disciple of Jesus Christ. I must go until Heaven returns, give until I drop, preach until all know, and work until He comes. And when He comes to get His own, He will have no problem recognizing me. My colours will be crystal clear!

Life Purpose

My Covenant

"Dear God, I totally give up all my plans and purposes, all my own desires and hopes. I accept Your will for my life. I give myself, my life, my all to You to be Yours forever. Fill me with Your Holy Spirit, use me as You will, send me where You will, work out Your whole will in my life at any cost, both now and forever."

Sign_____

Date_____

Used by permission from Alice Sneed. Thank you!

David Kalamen

About The Author

David is the founder of Kelowna Christian Center Society (KCCS) (www.kccsociety.ca) and has led its development for the last forty-two years. KCCS has experienced a profound growth in influence locally, provincially and globally through the numerous and varied ministries it has given birth to.

Life Purpose has become a life message that emerged from an experience David had with the Lord at nineteen years of age. After years of studying the Bible and years of testing the veracity of *Life Purpose*

Life Purpose

principles, what he shares will challenge your faith and obedience to rise to another level.

David is an international speaker who has been asked to teach this material globally to a very broad audience: through national television, on YWAM bases, at mainline denominational conferences, to Asian business leaders, in political forums, throughout North America but also in Communist countries like China, Vietnam, and Cuba, in small and large settings, through translators in many different cultures and languages – Taiwan, Russia, Nigeria, Mexico, and so on.

David's passion is to help people connect with their life calling, identify the seasons of life they are in, and help them fulfill the assignments God has for them, becoming a partner with God in making history. He confidently conveys that the will of God is knowable and doable, that God is no respecter of persons, and that all of us have a race that is completable.

Those who have listened to this teaching and applied themselves to live these principles out in their daily life, have seen their *Life Purpose* more clearly defined and their life activated to see and serve the purpose of God in their generation.

A secondary book, *A Sequel to Life Purpose*, is in the process of being written. In it the *Life Purpose* principles are applied to biblical personalities – ie. their call, their giftings, and their life story. The Romans 8:28 passage is explored to detail why things went well with some and why they did not with others.

A *Life Purpose Study Guide* is available for study groups who want to explore these principles personally, to see how their life purpose can intersect and interact with God's eternal purpose.

Life Purpose is a journey every believer is called to engage: its focus is to know God, to know ourselves, to know our calling, and to understand what next steps look like so that we can with joy faithfully complete our life story within His-Story.

Life Purpose

STUDY GUIDE

Connect with David at his website
www.davidkalamen.com

Manufactured by Amazon.ca
Bolton, ON

43991043R00175